December 25, 1998

To Mary Ann —

Hope you enjoy cooking these recipes as much as we loved creating them —

Fondly,
Barbara King

Merry Christmas!

Reflections Under the Sun

The Brightest Collection of Recipes from the Junior League of Phoenix

Reflections Under the Sun

*Copyright © 1999
Junior League of Phoenix, Inc.
P.O. Box 10223
Phoenix, Arizona 85064*

*Cover Recipe: Raspberry Tart
by Vincent Guerithault
Vincent's on Camelback*

*Cover Photography by
William McKellar Photography*

*Library of Congress Catalog Number: 98-067392
ISBN: 0-9613174-2-6*

*Edited, Designed and Manufactured by Favorite Recipes® Press
an imprint of*

FRP™

P.O. Box 305142, Nashville, Tennessee 37230, (800) 358-0560

*Manufactured in the United States of America
First Printing: 1999   15,000 copies*

Table of Contents

Recipes in this book are categorized by contributing source.

Something New Under the Sun

Fiesta Under the Sun

Desert Treasures

New Recipe for Reflections Under the Sun

Chef Recipe

Wine suggestions have been listed with entrée recipes. Most of the selections can be found at your local liquor store, while others are available at specialty wine merchants. We have provided general recommendations and encourage you to select wines according to your personal taste.

Cookbook Creation Committee

Robin Rodie Vitols-Chairman

Cay Cowie-Sustaining Advisor

Mary Budd Baroni

Megan Congleton

Becki Deem

Alice Henderson

Jeannette Hollander

Carrie Hulburd

Holly Larsen

Nancy Roach

Rebecca Rodie

Elizabeth Saba

Stephanie Scott

Cary Thomas

Chefs

Anton Braunbauer	Hyatt Regency Scottsdale
Tammie Coe	Desert Highlands
Michael de Maria	Michael's
Robert DeSantis	Samaritan Health Systems
Carol Ellis	Arcadia Farms
Barbara Pool Fenzl	Les Gourmettes Cooking School
Reed Groban	Scottsdale Princess
Christopher Gross	Christopher and Paola's Fermier Brasserie
Vincent Guerithault	Vincent's on Camelback
Edward Hartwig	Samaritan Health Systems
Tim Hoobler	Desert Highlands
Linda Hopkins	Les Petites Gourmettes
Erasmo Kamnitzer	Razz's Restaurant

Eddie Matney	Eddie Matney's Epicurian Trio
James McDevitt	Restaurant Hapa
Mary Jo "Mama Jo" McDonald	KEZ Radio
Robert McGrath	The Roaring Fork
Donna Nordin	Café Terra Cotta
Roland Oberholzer	Roland's
Patrick Ponce Poblete	Lon's at Hermosa Inn
Rick Sederholt	Remington's Restaurant at The Scottsdale Plaza Resort
Alessandro Stratta	The Phoenician
Mark Tarbell	Tarbell's
Robert Trick	House of Tricks
Scott Tompkins	Marco Polo Café
Roy Yamaguchi	Roy's

Introduction

The Junior League of Phoenix has been brightening the Valley of the Sun for more than six decades. The warm embrace of the Junior League of Phoenix is possible thanks to monies raised by fundraisers, like this cookbook.

Reflections Under the Sun represents the fourth cookbook published by the Junior League of Phoenix. Growing demand for our earlier, out-of-print books led to development of this "favorites" collection. Shining recipes from *Something New Under the Sun*, *Fiesta Under the Sun*, and *Desert Treasures* all have been included. In addition, you will find fabulous new contributions from our current membership and Valley of the Sun chefs. This compilation offers the best of the past and hot new trends in cuisine.

Thanks to your purchase of *Reflections Under the Sun*, the Junior League of Phoenix is able to continue its long tradition of community service through trained voluntarism. Our 1,300 members have risen to meet countless needs within Metropolitan Phoenix. A sampling of our past and current programs is listed below.

The Junior League of Phoenix's most enlightened dreams become a reality because of dedicated volunteers and successful fundraisers.

Reflections Under the Sun promises to be our brightest cookbook to date. This book is offered to you as a reflection of our warm hospitality.

Programs of the Junior League of Phoenix:

Arizona Science Center

Crisis Nursery

Emily Anderson Family Learning Center

Golden Gate Settlement

Heard Museum

Immunization Saturday

Orpheum Theatre Renovation

Phoenix Art Museum

Phoenix Museum of History

Phoenix Zoo Education Center

Race for the Cure—Breast Cancer Research—Phoenix

Ronald McDonald House

Rosson House

Teen Outreach

Transitional Housing for Homeless Families

Volunteer Center

...and many more

Menus

Cinco de Mayo Celebration

Chips and Salsa
Tortilla Soup, 39
Beach-Style Carne Asada, 96
Green Chile Pilaf, 150
Chocolate Citrus Cake, 156
or
Fresh Fruit and Lucy's Lace Cookies, 180

Grande Classics

Classic Pâté, 21
Stuffed Brie, 16
Calcutta Mulligatawny Soup, 37
Hearts of Palm with Tangy Lemon Dressing, 74
or
A Traditional Caesar Salad
Preston's Chateaubriand, 94
Bread Pudding with Drunken Sauce, 169

East Meets West

Coconut Tiger Shrimp Sticks with Thai Cocktail Sauce, 25
Mandarin Salad with Raspberry Vinaigrette, 80
Waikiki Ribs, 103
or
Oriental Leg of Lamb, 100
or
Chinese Pork Tenderloins, 102
Pacific Wave Wild Rice, 152
Huggo's Asian Mushrooms, 146
Coconut Caramel Ring, 173
or
Fairy Pie, 160

Fiesta Bowl Bash

Fiesta Dip, 28
Marge's Mexican Salad, 77
Green Chile Beef Stew, 47
or
Mexican Lasagna, 98
Cowboy Caramel Corn, 183
Oatmeal Carmelitas, 181

Social Swirl

Garlic Custards, 18
Cool Bleu Dressing, 91 with
Snow Peas, Hearts of Palm and Belgian Endive for Dipping
Scrumptious Stuffed Mushrooms, 21
Gift Mart Nuts, 31
Zesty Hot Crab Dip, 27
Walnut Feta Canapés, 31
Teriyaki Beef Tenderloin, 95, Sliced and
Served with Rolls and Appropriate Condiments
Grand Chocolate Mint Squares, 177
Pecan Puffs, 182

Shower Supreme

Cold Tomato Bisque, 43
or
Spinach Garden Vegetable Salad, 79
Dilly Bread, 56
Chicken Phyllo Casserole, 107
Chilled Asparagus Salad, 66
Lemon Almond Tart, 162

Dining au Deux

Cold Smoked Rock Shrimp with Plum Tomato Relish, 24
Pear and Bleu Cheese Salad, 81
Veal Chops with Cognac Cream Sauce, 105
Fresh Asparagus or Broccoli
Vincent's Crème Brûleé in Sweet Taco Shells, 168

Friends in the Kitchen

Arizona Crab Cakes, 24
Baked Goat Cheese and Garlic Spread, 30
Fresh Italian Bread
Ultimate Caesar Salad, 75
Pasta with Scallops and Lemony Mustard Sauce, 126
Chocolate Malakoff, 165

Grilling Poolside

Monterey Cheese Spread, 29
Coyote Caviar, 26
Roy's Kula Onion and Tomato Salad, 68
and
Grilled Margarita Chicken, 110
or
French Green Bean Salad, 69
and
Grilled Tuna with Spinach and Tomatoes, 123
Vanilla Bean Ice Cream Topped with Lemon Dessert Sauce, 171
Ginger Chews, 179

Orange Blossom Brunch

Raspberry Muffins with Streusel, 52
Fruit and Spinach Salad, 79
Springtime Quiche, 59
or
Lemon Cream Chicken, 110
Pink Grapefruit and Champagne Sorbet, 171
or
Frozen Chambord Torte with Raspberry Sauce, 172

Tour D'Italia

Grilled Portobello Mushrooms with Pesto and Goat Cheese, 20
or
Rosemary Pizza with Onion, Goat Cheese and Pecans, 23
Salad Primavera with Citrus Caper Dressing, 78
Tuscan Salmon, 120
or
Piccata con Carciofi, 104
Almond Black Bottom Cheesecake, 158

Holiday Memories

Gift Mart Nuts, 31
Stuffed Brie, 16
Spinach Salad with Chutney Dressing, 77
Easy and Elegant Rack of Lamb, 100
or
Your Favorite Roasted Turkey
Sage and Wild Rice Stuffing with Kahlúa, 151
Company Carrots, 139
Festive Fruit Compote with Cranberries, 153
Musician's Tart, 163
or
Holiday Cake with Hard Sauce, 157

Appetizers

Artichoke Parmesan Rounds

1 (10-count) can flaky rolls or biscuits
³/₄ cup mayonnaise
³/₄ cup grated Parmesan cheese
¹/₂ teaspoon onion juice
1 (4-ounce) can artichoke hearts,
drained, sliced
Paprika

Separate each roll into 4 pieces. Place the pieces ¹/₂ inch apart on a nonstick baking sheet. Combine the mayonnaise, Parmesan cheese and onion juice in a small bowl; mix well. Spread a spoonful of the mayonnaise mixture on each piece of dough. Top with a slice of artichoke heart. Spread the artichoke with another spoonful of the mayonnaise mixture. Sprinkle paprika over the top. Bake at 400 degrees for 10 to 12 minutes or until golden brown.

Serves 12 to 18

A party hit.

Stuffed Brie

1 (4-ounce) round of Brie cheese
3 ounces cream cheese, softened
3 tablespoons crumbled bleu cheese
1 to 2 tablespoons dry sherry
2 tablespoons sliced almonds
¹/₄ cup sliced grapes

Slice the Brie round in half horizontally. Combine the cream cheese, bleu cheese and sherry in a small bowl; mix until well combined but not smooth. Reserve a few almonds and grapes for garnish. Fold the rest into the cheese mixture. Spread the mixture on the bottom half of the Brie. Cover with the top half. Garnish with reserved almonds and grapes. Cut into wedges. Serve the cheese at room temperature.

Serves 6 to 8

Looks beautiful served on a tray filled with assorted crackers and lots of red and green grapes.

Crab and Pine Nut Cakes

Anton Braunbauer
Hyatt Regency Scottsdale

4 slices white bread, torn into small pieces
1/2 cup milk
1/2 cup pine nuts
2 tablespoons mayonnaise
2 tablespoons Worcestershire sauce
2 tablespoons chopped parsley
2 tablespoons baking powder
2 tablespoons Old Bay seasoning
2 eggs, beaten
2 pounds crab meat
Salt and pepper to taste
Oil for sautéing

Moisten the bread with the milk in a bowl. Add the pine nuts, mayonnaise, Worcestershire sauce, parsley, baking powder, Old Bay seasoning, eggs, crab meat, salt and pepper; mix well. Shape into cakes. Heat the oil in a large skillet over medium-high heat. Sauté the cakes until golden brown on both sides.

Serves 2

Mary's Crab Mousse

1 (10-ounce) can cream of mushroom or cream of celery soup
1 envelope unflavored gelatin
1/4 cup cold water
6 to 7 ounces crab meat
1/2 to 3/4 cup chopped celery
1 cup mayonnaise
1/2 cup chopped onion
8 ounces cream cheese, softened
1 (2-ounce) jar pimentos, drained

Heat the soup in a saucepan over medium heat. Soften the gelatin in the cold water. Combine the soup, gelatin, crab meat, celery, mayonnaise, onion, cream cheese and pimentos in a large bowl; mix thoroughly. Transfer the mixture to a decorative mold. Chill or freeze until firm. Serve with sesame crackers.

Serves 8

Garlic Custards

Donna Nordin
Café Terra Cotta

*2 tablespoons roasted garlic
(see page 106)
1 jalapeño, minced
2 cups heavy cream
4 egg yolks, beaten
2 eggs, beaten
³/₄ teaspoon salt
¹/₄ teaspoon white pepper
¹/₈ teaspoon nutmeg
¹/₄ cup red wine vinegar*

*³/₄ cup olive oil
1 teaspoon Dijon mustard
1 cup salsa
2 tablespoons butter
1 cup toasted hazelnuts
¹/₄ teaspoon dried oregano, crushed
¹/₄ teaspoon dried thyme, crushed
¹/₈ teaspoon cayenne
¹/₈ teaspoon ground cumin, or to taste
Salt and black pepper to taste*

Butter eight 4-ounce ramekins. Mix the roasted garlic, jalapeño, whipping cream, egg yolks, eggs, salt, white pepper and nutmeg in a mixer bowl. Pour the cream mixture into the ramekins. Place the prepared ramekins in a baking pan. Place the baking pan on the middle rack of the oven. Add hot water to come halfway up the sides of the ramekins. Bake at 300 degrees for 45 to 50 minutes or until a knife inserted in the center of the custards come out clean. Remove the pan from the oven. Let the custards stand in the hot water for up to 20 minutes to keep warm. Combine the wine vinegar, oil, Dijon mustard and salsa in a saucepan over low heat; whisk until well mixed. Set aside and keep warm. Melt the butter in a skillet over medium-high heat. Add the hazelnuts, oregano, thyme, cayenne, cumin, salt and black pepper. Sauté until the nuts are coated. Remove to a cutting board and chop coarsely. Turn the custards out of ramekins onto individual serving plates. Spoon warm vinaigrette over each. Sprinkle with additional hazelnuts. Can substitute walnuts, pecans or mixed nuts for the hazelnuts.

Serves 8

Rich and addictive!

Appetizers

Goat Cheese Torte

1 1/2 cups butter, softened
8 ounces cream cheese, softened
8 ounces goat cheese, softened
1 cup prepared pesto
1 cup drained and minced sun-dried tomatoes

Cream the butter, cream cheese and goat cheese in a mixer bowl until light and fluffy. Spread 1/3 of the mixture in the bottom of a small springform pan or decorative bowl. Spread 1/2 of the pesto over the cheese mixture. Continue layering the cheese mixture and pesto mixture, ending with the cheese mixture. Spread the sun-dried tomatoes over the top. Chill for at least 1 hour. Unmold and serve at room temperature with sliced baguettes or crackers.

Serves 12 to 16

Mushroom Mousse

2 tablespoons butter
1 pound mushrooms, minced
8 ounces cream cheese, softened
1 teaspoon garlic salt
1 1/2 teaspoons minced green bell pepper
1/8 teaspoon hot pepper sauce
1/4 teaspoon Worcestershire sauce

Heat the butter in a large skillet over medium-high heat. Add the mushrooms. Sauté until no liquid remains and the mushrooms start to brown. Combine the mushrooms, cream cheese, garlic salt, green pepper, pepper sauce and Worcestershire sauce in the bowl of a food processor. Process until smooth. Transfer to a decorative mold or bowl. Chill for 24 hours.

Serves 8 to 12

Chopped parsley pressed on the outside of the shaped mousse makes a beautiful presentation.

Grilled Portobello Mushrooms

with Pesto and Goat Cheese

Robert Trick
House of Tricks

6 portobello mushrooms,
stems removed
1/4 cup olive oil
1/2 teaspoon salt
1/2 teaspoon freshly ground pepper
2/3 cup chopped fresh cilantro
1/2 cup olive oil
1/3 cup grated Parmesan cheese
1/3 cup toasted pine nuts

2 cloves of garlic, minced
1 teaspoon fresh lime juice
1/8 teaspoon salt
1/8 teaspoon freshly ground pepper
2 Roma tomatoes, sliced into
thin wedges
1 cup mild goat cheese
2 tablespoons balsamic vinegar
1 teaspoon soy sauce

Place the mushrooms skin side down on a nonstick baking sheet. Brush 1/4 cup oil over the mushrooms. Sprinkle with 1/2 teaspoon salt and 1/2 teaspoon pepper. Bake at 400 degrees for 15 minutes or until soft. Combine the cilantro, 1/2 cup oil, Parmesan cheese, pine nuts, garlic, lime juice, 1/8 teaspoon salt and 1/8 teaspoon pepper in a food processor container. Process until well blended. Spoon the mixture over the mushrooms. Arrange the tomato wedges in a spiral design over each mushroom. Dot with goat cheese. Broil on high for 2 minutes or until the goat cheese begins to color. Remove from the broiler. Combine the vinegar and soy sauce in a small bowl; mix well. Drizzle vinegar mixture over the mushrooms.

Serves 6

Appetizers

Scrumptious Stuffed

Mushrooms

1 pound mushrooms
1 cup butter
3 tablespoons chopped green bell pepper
1/4 cup reconstituted dried onion
4 cups fresh bread crumbs
3 tablespoons minced chives
1 teaspoon salt
1/4 teaspoon pepper

Remove and finely chop the mushroom stems; reserve. Melt the butter in a skillet over medium-high heat. Add the green pepper and onion; mix well. Add the reserved mushroom stems. Sauté for 10 minutes or until tender. Remove from the heat. Add the bread crumbs, chives, salt and pepper; mix well. Adjust seasonings. Place the mushroom caps skin side down on a nonstick baking sheet. Fill each cap with the stuffing mixture, mounding it in the center. Bake at 350 degrees for 15 minutes.

Serves 24

Terrific as an appetizer or side dish.

Classic Pâté

1/4 teaspoon unflavored gelatin
1/4 cup water
1/4 cup condensed consommé
12 ounces chicken livers
3/4 cup butter, softened
3 tablespoons minced onion
1/4 teaspoon salt
1/4 teaspoon nutmeg
1/4 teaspoon anchovy paste
1 teaspoon dry mustard
1/8 teaspoon cayenne
1/8 teaspoon ground cloves

Soften the gelatin in the water. Combine the consommé and gelatin in a saucepan over medium heat. Cook until the gelatin is dissolved, stirring constantly. Pour into a 2 1/2- to 3-cup mold. Chill for 1 hour or until firm. Place the livers in a saucepan over medium-high heat. Cover with water. Bring to a boil. Reduce the heat. Simmer for 20 minutes. Cool slightly; drain. Combine the livers and butter in a blender container. Process until the mixture is smooth. Add the onion, salt, nutmeg, anchovy paste, mustard, cayenne and cloves. Process until well mixed. Spread mixture over molded gelatin. Chill, covered, until firm.

Serves 12 to 20

Pâté en Croute

2¹/4 cups flour
¹/2 teaspoon salt
³/4 cup butter, cut into small pieces
1 egg
3 tablespoons sour cream
¹/4 cup butter
1 pound each ground beef, ground veal
and ground pork

1 cup minced mushrooms
¹/2 cup minced onion
¹/4 cup chopped parsley
1 cup shredded Gruyère cheese
2 eggs
¹/4 cup milk
Salt and pepper to taste
2 tablespoons heavy cream

Sift the flour and ¹/2 teaspoon salt into a mixer bowl. Make a well in the center. Add ³/4 cup butter, 1 egg and sour cream. Mix until a smooth dough forms. Wrap in plastic wrap. Chill for 30 minutes. Melt ¹/4 cup butter in a skillet over medium-high heat. Add the ground beef, ground veal and ground pork. Cook until the meats are crumbly, stirring occasionally; drain well. Transfer the mixture to a large mixer bowl. Add the mushrooms, onion, parsley, Gruyère cheese, 2 eggs, milk, salt and pepper; mix well. Roll the dough into a 10x15-inch rectangle. Cut and reserve a 10x5-inch piece. Fit the remaining dough into a 5x9-inch loaf pan. Place the meat mixture in the pan. Cover with the reserved dough. Moisten the edges and pinch them together to seal. Brush the top with cream. Bake at 375 degrees for 45 minutes or until golden brown.

Serves 8

Delicious hot or cold. Can be frozen.

Rosemary Pizza with

Onion, Goat Cheese and Pecans

Linda Hopkins
Les Petites Gourmettes

2 teaspoons dry yeast
2 cups warm water
$^1/_4$ teaspoon sugar
$^1/_2$ cup olive oil
5 to 5$^1/_4$ cups flour
2 tablespoons chopped fresh rosemary
1 tablespoon salt

2 pounds onions, thinly sliced
$^1/_4$ cup unsalted butter
12 ounces goat cheese, crumbled
$^3/_4$ cup pecan pieces
1 tablespoon chopped fresh rosemary
Salt and pepper to taste

Combine the yeast, $^1/_4$ cup of the water and sugar in a small bowl. Let stand for 5 minutes or until foamy. Combine 2 tablespoons of the oil, remaining water, yeast mixture and 3 cups of the flour in a large mixer bowl; stir until flour is moistened. Beat for 2 minutes on medium speed. Add 2 tablespoons rosemary, 2 cups of the remaining flour and 1 tablespoon salt. Beat for 2 minutes on low speed or until a soft, sticky dough forms, adding remaining flour if needed. Knead on a floured surface for 1 minute. Transfer to a lightly oiled bowl, turning to coat. Let rise, covered with plastic wrap, in a warm place for 1 hour or until doubled in bulk. Oil a pizza pan with 2 tablespoons of the oil. Punch down the dough. Pat into the pan. Let rise for 40 minutes or until doubled in bulk. Sauté the onions in the butter in a skillet over medium-high heat for 20 minutes or until caramelized. Let stand to cool. Sprinkle the caramelized onions, goat cheese, pecans, 1 tablespoon rosemary, salt and pepper over the prepared dough. Drizzle with the remaining $^1/_4$ cup oil. Bake at 450 degrees for 20 minutes or until golden brown.

Serves 8

Appetizers

Arizona Crab Cakes

1/4 cup freshly squeezed lime juice
2 1/2 cups crab meat
1/2 cup minced green onions
1/2 cup minced cilantro
1/4 cup chopped green chiles
1/2 cup mayonnaise
1/2 teaspoon crushed red pepper flakes
1 tablespoon Dijon mustard
3/4 cup bread crumbs
1/4 cup olive oil
2 tablespoons unsalted butter

Drizzle the lime juice over the crab meat in a mixer bowl. Add green onions, cilantro and green chiles; mix lightly with a fork. Combine the mayonnaise, red pepper and Dijon mustard in a small bowl; mix well. Add to the crab mixture; mix well. Add 1/2 cup of the bread crumbs; mix well. If necessary, add more bread crumbs, 1 tablespoon at a time, stirring until the mixture sticks together. Form into ten 2 1/2-inch cakes 3/4 inch thick. Chill, covered with plastic wrap, for 30 minutes. Heat the oil and butter in a large skillet over medium-high heat. Coat the crab cakes with the remaining bread crumbs. Cook the crab cakes for 3 to 5 minutes on each side or until golden brown.

Serves 6

Cold Smoked Rock Shrimp with Plum Tomato Relish

Mark Tarbell
Tarbell's

1 1/4 pounds rock shrimp
3 Roma tomatoes, chopped
1/4 cup chopped onion
1/4 bunch cilantro, chopped
1 tablespoon tomato paste
1 or 2 serrano chiles, chopped
1/4 teaspoon hot pepper sauce
Kosher salt to taste
1/4 cup freshly squeezed lime juice

Prepare a smoker with 4 ounces of apple wood chips according to the manufacturer's directions. Fill a small aluminum baking pan with ice. Remove the rack and place the pan on top of the wood chips. Replace the rack. Place the shrimp on the rack. Smoke for 7 to 10 minutes. Remove to an ovenproof pan. Bake at 350 degrees for 10 minutes or until cooked through. Mix the remaining ingredients in a bowl. Spoon the relish in a circle onto a serving plate. Top with shrimp. Serve immediately.

Serves 6

A wonderful first course.

Coconut Tiger Shrimp Sticks

With Thai Cocktail Sauce

Roy Yamaguchi
Roy's

2 cups catsup
¹/₂ cup packed light brown sugar
¹/₄ cup chili sauce
2 tablespoons fish sauce
2 tablespoons soy sauce
2 tablespoons rice wine vinegar
¹/₂ cup freshly squeezed lime juice
¹/₂ cup chopped cilantro
4 large Kaffir lime leaves, minced
(available in Asian markets)

1 stalk lemon grass, minced
1 cup chopped fresh mint
16 large tiger prawns, peeled, deveined
1 cup coconut flakes
1 cup panko bread crumbs
(available in Asian markets)
1 cup flour
4 eggs, beaten
3 cups vegetable oil

Mix the catsup, brown sugar, chili sauce, fish sauce, soy sauce, wine vinegar, lime juice, cilantro, lime leaves, lemon grass and mint in a large bowl. Cover and chill thoroughly. Place the prawns on bamboo skewers starting at the tail and running through to the head. Mix the coconut and panko together. Coat the prawns with the flour, dip into the eggs and coat with the coconut mixture. Heat the oil in a large skillet over medium-high heat. Cook the shrimp sticks a few at a time in the oil until cooked through and golden brown. Drain on paper towels. Spoon the sauce onto the center of a plate. Arrange the shrimp sticks around the rim of the plate. Garnish with additional cilantro.

Serves 4

Appetizers

Coyote Caviar

1 (15-ounce) can black beans, drained, rinsed
1 (4-ounce) can chopped black olives, drained
1/4 cup chopped onion
1 (4-ounce) can chopped green chiles
1 clove of garlic, chopped
1/4 cup chopped cilantro
2 tablespoons vegetable oil
2 tablespoons freshly squeezed lime juice
2 teaspoons chili powder
1/4 teaspoon salt
1/4 teaspoon crushed red pepper flakes
1/4 teaspoon cumin
1 teaspoon black pepper
8 ounces cream cheese, softened
2 hard-cooked eggs, peeled, chopped
Salsa to taste
1 green onion, sliced

Combine the black beans, black olives, onion, green chiles, garlic, cilantro, oil, lime juice, chili powder, salt, red pepper, cumin and black pepper in a bowl; mix well. Chill, covered, for 2 hours. Spread the cream cheese on a round serving plate. Cover with the black bean mixture. Arrange the eggs and salsa around the edge of the black bean mixture. Sprinkle with the green onion. Serve with tortilla chips.

Serves 12

A very Southwestern appetizer. Sure to be a hit.

Appetizers

Zesty Hot Crab Dip

1 (7-ounce) can crab meat
8 ounces cream cheese, softened
1 teaspoon dry vermouth
2 tablespoons chopped onion
1/2 teaspoon prepared horseradish
1/4 teaspoon salt
1/8 teaspoon cayenne pepper
1/8 teaspoon hot pepper sauce
1 teaspoon dillweed
1/8 teaspoon Worcestershire sauce
1/2 cup sliced almonds

Rinse the crab meat. Pick over and discard any pieces of shell. Combine the crab meat, cream cheese, vermouth, onion, horseradish, salt, cayenne, pepper sauce, dillweed and Worcestershire sauce in a bowl; mix well. Spoon into a 2-cup ovenproof dish. Cover with almonds. Bake at 375 degrees for 15 minutes. Serve with toasted baguette slices.

Serves 8

Warm Bleu Cheese and Bacon Dip

7 slices bacon, chopped
2 cloves of garlic, minced
8 ounces cream cheese, softened
1/4 cup half-and-half
1 cup crumbled bleu cheese
2 tablespoons chopped fresh chives

Cook bacon in a large skillet over medium-high heat until almost crisp; drain well. Add the garlic. Cook until the bacon is crisp and the garlic is golden brown. Beat the cream cheese in a mixer bowl until creamy. Add the half-and-half; mix well. Add the bacon mixture, bleu cheese and chives; mix well. Transfer to a 2-cup ovenproof dish. Cover with foil. Bake at 350 degrees for 30 minutes. Serve warm with sliced baguette or sliced apples.

Serves 4 to 6

Fiesta Dip

1 (16-ounce) can refried beans
1 (4-ounce) can chopped green chiles
2 cups sour cream
1 tomato, chopped
2 (6-ounce) cans frozen avocado dip, thawed
$^1/_2$ cup chopped red onion
1 (4-ounce) can chopped black olives
1 cup shredded Cheddar cheese

Layer the refried beans, green chiles, sour cream, tomato, avocado dip, onion, black olives and cheese on a 12-inch plate. Place the plate on a larger serving plate. Surround with large tostado chips.

Serves 12 to 16

Men love this!

Curry Vegetable Dip

2 cups mayonnaise
3 tablespoons catsup
3 packets artificial sweetener
1 tablespoon freshly squeezed lemon juice
3 drops hot pepper sauce
2 teaspoons curry powder
3 tablespoons minced onion

Combine the mayonnaise, catsup, sweetener, lemon juice, pepper sauce, curry powder and onion in a bowl; mix well. Chill until ready to serve. Serve with fresh vegetables.

Serves 16

Appetizers

Garlic Feta Cheese Spread

1 clove of garlic, minced
1/4 teaspoon salt
8 ounces feta cheese, crumbled
1/2 cup mayonnaise
1/4 teaspoon dried marjoram, crushed
1/4 teaspoon dried dillweed
1/4 teaspoon dried thyme, crushed
1/2 teaspoon chopped fresh basil, or to taste
12 ounces cream cheese, softened,
cut into cubes

Mash the garlic and salt together until of a paste consistency. Combine the garlic paste, feta cheese, mayonnaise, marjoram, dillweed, thyme, basil and cream cheese in the bowl of a food processor. Process until smooth. Transfer the mixture to a crock or ramekin. Chill, covered, for 2 hours. May refrigerate for up to 1 week.

Serves 6

Try this delicious spread on baked or mashed potatoes.

Monterey Cheese Spread

2 pounds Monterey Jack cheese, shredded
1 (4-ounce) can chopped green chiles
1 (4-ounce) can chopped black olives
4 tomatoes, chopped
1 bunch green onions, chopped
1/4 cup chopped fresh parsley
1 (8-ounce) bottle Italian-style salad dressing

Combine the cheese, green chiles, black olives, tomatoes, green onions, parsley and salad dressing in a bowl; mix well. Chill for 4 hours. Serve with wheat thins, bagel chips or tortilla chips.

Serves 24

A favorite for all ages.

Baked Goat Cheese and

Garlic Spread

12 cloves of garlic, peeled
1 tablespoon vegetable oil
2 tablespoons butter
1 red onion, thinly sliced
1 tablespoon light brown sugar
10 ounces goat cheese, crumbled
1 tablespoon balsamic vinegar
Salt and pepper to taste
1/4 cup chopped fresh basil

Place the garlic in an ovenproof dish. Drizzle with oil. Bake, covered, at 350 degrees for 30 minutes or until the cloves are soft. Remove to a rack and let cool. Melt the butter in a skillet over medium-high heat. Add the onion. Sauté until golden brown. Add the brown sugar. Cook until the brown sugar is dissolved, stirring constantly. Remove from the heat. Let cool. Spread the onion mixture in an 8x8-inch ovenproof dish. Sprinkle with the goat cheese. Arrange the garlic over the top. Bake at 350 degrees for 25 minutes or until the cheese is melted but not bubbly. Add the vinegar, salt and pepper; mix well. Transfer to a serving bowl. Sprinkle basil over the top. Serve warm or at room temperature with baguette slices.

Serves 6

Can be prepared one day ahead and baked just prior to serving.

Walnut Feta Canapés

1 1/3 cups feta cheese
3 tablespoons safflower oil or vegetable oil
3/4 cup soy milk or regular milk
2 1/2 cups chopped walnuts
1/4 teaspoon cayenne
1/2 teaspoon hot pepper sauce
1 teaspoon paprika

Combine 1/3 cup of the feta cheese, 1 tablespoon of the oil, 1/4 cup of the milk and 1/2 cup of the walnuts in a blender container. Process on low speed just until mixed. Process on medium speed until the mixture is smooth. Add the remaining feta cheese, oil, milk and walnuts with the blender running. Add the cayenne, pepper sauce and paprika. Process until a creamy paste forms. Transfer to a serving bowl. Chill for 1 hour. Spread on toasted baguette slices or on toasted pita bread. May serve as a dip with fresh vegetables.

Serves 8 to 12

Gift Mart Nuts

1 cup packed light brown sugar
1 teaspoon salt
1 teaspoon cinnamon
1/2 teaspoon allspice
1/4 teaspoon nutmeg
1/4 teaspoon ground cloves
3 tablespoons water
3 cups walnut or pecan halves

Combine the brown sugar, salt, cinnamon, allspice, nutmeg, cloves and water in a microwave-safe bowl; mix well. Microwave on High for 3 minutes. Add the walnuts; mix well. Microwave on High for 5 minutes. Spread on a baking sheet to cool completely.

Serves 12

Serve alone or tossed in a green salad with bleu cheese.

Soups & Chilis

Albondigas Soup

2 quarts chicken broth
1 (28-ounce) can chopped tomatoes
1 tablespoon vegetable oil
1 clove of garlic, minced
$^1/_2$ cup chopped onion
1 green chile, seeded, chopped
1 teaspoon chili powder
$^1/_4$ teaspoon dried oregano
$^1/_2$ teaspoon coarsely ground
black pepper

1 teaspoon salt
3 sprigs cilantro, chopped
1 pound ground beef
1 egg, beaten
2 tablespoons white rice, uncooked
1 tablespoon flour
1 green chile, seeded, chopped
$^1/_2$ teaspoon oregano
$^1/_2$ teaspoon onion salt

Combine the chicken broth and tomatoes in a 4-quart saucepan over high heat. Heat the oil in a skillet over medium-high heat. Add the garlic, onion and 1 green chile. Sauté until the onion is soft. Add the sautéed vegetables to the broth. Bring to a boil. Remove $^1/_2$ cup of broth; add the chili powder and mix thoroughly. Return the mixture to the soup. Stir in $^1/_4$ teaspoon oregano, black pepper, salt and cilantro. Simmer the soup for 15 minutes. Combine the ground beef, egg, rice, flour, 1 green chile, $^1/_2$ teaspoon oregano and onion salt in a bowl; mix thoroughly. Shape into 1$^1/_2$-inch meatballs. Add the meatballs a few at a time to the simmering soup. Cook for 20 minutes or until the meatballs are cooked through. Serve immediately.

Serves 16 to 20

A Mexican favorite.

Cream of Artichoke and

Mushroom Soup

$^1/_4$ cup butter
2 tablespoons finely chopped onion
$^1/_2$ cup sliced mushrooms
$^1/_4$ cup flour
1 (10-ounce) can chicken broth
2 cups half-and-half
1 (10-ounce) can artichokes, drained,
chopped
$^1/_2$ teaspoon salt
Cracked pepper to taste

Melt the butter in a saucepan over medium-high heat. Add the onion and mushrooms. Sauté for 5 minutes. Stir in the flour. Cook slowly for 2 minutes, stirring constantly. Add the broth and half-and-half. Cook until thickened, stirring occasionally. Add the artichokes and salt; mix well. Transfer half the soup to a blender container. Process until smooth. Return to the saucepan. Cook until heated through. Ladle into soup bowls and sprinkle with cracked pepper before serving.

Serves 6 to 8

This soup can be made in advance and reheated.

Mexican Corn Chowder

1 cup chopped onion
2 to 3 cloves of garlic, minced
2 tablespoons butter
2 tablespoons flour
2 (12-ounce) packages frozen corn
kernels, thawed
$1^1/_3$ cups chicken broth
$^1/_4$ cup chopped fresh parsley
1 (4-ounce) can chopped green chiles
2 cups 2% milk
1 teaspoon salt
$^1/_2$ teaspoon freshly ground pepper
$^1/_4$ teaspoon oregano

Sauté the onions and garlic in the butter in a saucepan over medium-high heat for 3 to 5 minutes or until the onions are soft. Add the flour. Cook for 2 minutes or until bubbly, stirring constantly. Add half the corn, half the broth, half the parsley and the green chiles; mix well. Process the mixture in a blender just until mixed. Return the mixture to the saucepan. Add the remaining corn, broth and parsley and milk, salt, pepper and oregano. Cook until heated through. Serve garnished with shredded Cheddar or Monterey Jack cheese, chopped tomatoes, chopped avocado, chopped cooked chicken and crumbled crisp-fried bacon with tortilla chips on the side.

Serves 4 to 6

Marvelous Minestrone

2 slices bacon, chopped
1 pound ground beef
1 cup chopped onion
1 clove of garlic, minced
1 cup chopped celery
1 (6-ounce) can tomato paste
1 beef bouillon cube
5 cups water
2 teaspoons sugar
1 teaspoon pepper
2 teaspoons salt
$1/2$ teaspoon oregano
$1/2$ cup uncooked macaroni
1 medium zucchini, chopped
5 ounces fresh spinach leaves
Grated Parmesan cheese to taste

Cook the bacon in a large saucepan over medium-high heat until crisp. Remove and reserve the bacon. Add the ground beef, onion and garlic to the pan. Cook, stirring frequently, until the ground beef is brown and crumbly; drain well. Add the celery, tomato paste, bouillon cube, water, sugar, pepper, salt and oregano; mix well. Bring to a boil. Reduce the heat. Simmer, covered, for 30 minutes. Add the macaroni; mix well. Cook, covered, for 10 minutes. Add the zucchini and spinach; stir. Cook for 5 minutes or until the macaroni is tender. Add the reserved bacon; mix well. Serve with Parmesan cheese on the side.

Serves 6

This recipe is easily doubled and reheats well.

Creamy Green Chile Soup

6 tablespoons unsalted butter
1 cup chopped onion
3 (4-ounce) cans chopped green chiles
2 (28-ounce) cans plum tomatoes, drained
12 ounces cream cheese
2 (14-ounce) cans chicken broth
3 cups half-and-half or 2 cups milk
2 tablespoons plus 2 teaspoons freshly
squeezed lemon juice
Cayenne pepper to taste

Melt the butter in a saucepan over medium-high heat. Add the onion. Sauté until the onion is soft. Add the green chiles and tomatoes. Cook for 8 to 10 minutes or until liquid is reduced. Add the cream cheese; mix well. Do not allow to boil. Add the broth, half-and-half and lemon juice; mix well. Ladle into soup bowls and sprinkle each with cayenne pepper. May serve warm or at room temperature.

Serves 12 to 16

Calcutta Mulligatawny Soup

3¹/₂ pounds chicken pieces
³/₄ cup flour
¹/₄ cup melted butter or margarine
1 cup chopped onion
1 cup chopped celery
1 cup chopped carrots
1 cup chopped tart apples
1 tablespoon curry powder
2 teaspoons salt
¹/₂ teaspoon ground mace
¹/₄ teaspoon pepper
¹/₄ teaspoon chili powder
¹/₂ cup flaked coconut
5 cups cold water or chicken broth

Coat the chicken with flour. Sauté the chicken in butter in a skillet over medium-high heat until brown on all sides. Push chicken to one side of the skillet. Add onions, celery, carrots, apples and any remaining flour; mix well. Cook for 5 minutes, stirring frequently. Stir in the remaining ingredients. Bring to a boil. Reduce the heat. Simmer, covered, for 1 hour. Remove and reserve the chicken. Simmer the soup, covered, for 1 hour; stirring frequently. Skim and discard the fat. Purée soup in a blender. Return to skillet. Remove the chicken from the bones. Add chicken to soup. Cook until heated through.

Serves 4 to 6

8700 Pumpkin Soup

1/4 cup butter
1/2 cup chopped onion
3 cloves of garlic, chopped
3 shallots, chopped
1/2 bunch green onions, chopped
1/2 teaspoon each cumin, oregano,
hot chili powder and cayenne pepper
1/4 cup flour
1 quart chicken broth, heated
1 tablespoon tomato paste
2 pounds pumpkin or any hard yellow squash,
peeled, seeded, chopped,
1/2 bunch of cilantro, chopped
1/4 cup milk

Melt the butter in a saucepan over medium-high heat. Add the onions, garlic, shallots, green onions, cumin, oregano, chili powder and cayenne pepper; mix well. Sauté until the onions are soft. Sprinkle the flour over the vegetables. Cook for 12 minutes, stirring constantly with a wooden spoon. Add the chicken broth, tomato paste, pumpkin and cilantro; mix well. Simmer until the squash is tender. Transfer the mixture to a blender container. Process until smooth. Return to the saucepan. Add the milk. Cook until heated through, stirring occasionally.

Serves 8

Garnish with sour cream and fried tortilla strips.

Harvest Wild Rice Soup

1/2 cup wild rice
1 tablespoon butter
3/4 cup chopped onion
3/4 cup chopped celery
1/3 cup chopped green bell pepper
12 ounces bacon, cooked, crumbled
3 (10-ounce) cans cream of mushroom soup
2 (10-ounce) cans chicken broth
2 1/2 soup cans water
1 tablespoon sherry
Salt and pepper to taste

Cook the rice according to the package directions. Melt the butter in a saucepan over medium-high heat. Add the onions, celery, green pepper; mix well. Sauté until the onions are soft. Add the bacon, soup, broth, water, sherry, salt and pepper; mix well. Cook until heated through, stirring occasionally.

Serves 8 to 10

Sopa del Gringo

1 (14-ounce) can tomatoes
1 (7-ounce) can green chiles, seeded, chopped
1/4 cup chopped onion
3 cups turkey broth, or
2 (10-ounce) cans chicken broth
1 tablespoon green chile salsa
3 cups chopped cooked turkey
2 cups cooked brown rice
1 (10-ounce) package frozen corn
kernels, thawed
3/4 teaspoon ground cumin
1/2 teaspoon salt
1/2 teaspoon garlic salt
1/4 teaspoon chili powder

Combine the undrained tomatoes, green chiles and onion in a blender container. Process until smooth. Transfer to a 4-quart saucepan. Add the broth and salsa. Bring to a boil. Add the turkey, rice, corn, cumin, salt, garlic salt and chili powder; mix well. Cook over medium-high heat until heated through. Garnish with chopped cilantro or green onions.

Serves 12 to 16

This is a delicious way to use leftover holiday turkey.

Tortilla Soup

1/2 cup chopped onion
1 clove of garlic, minced
1 (4-ounce) can chopped green chiles
3 tablespoons vegetable oil
1 (10-ounce) can chicken broth
1 (10-ounce) can beef broth
1 1/2 cups tomato juice
1 1/2 cups water
1 large tomato, chopped
1 teaspoon cumin
2 tablespoons chili powder
1 teaspoon salt
1 cup fresh corn kernels (optional)
Chopped cooked chicken (optional)
4 to 6 corn tortillas, cut into 1-inch strips
1/4 cup shredded Monterey Jack or
Cheddar cheese

Sauté the onion, garlic and green chiles in 2 tablespoons oil in a saucepan over medium-high heat until onion is soft. Add broths, tomato juice, water, tomato, cumin, chili powder, salt, corn and chicken. Bring to a boil. Reduce the heat. Simmer for 1 hour. Stir-fry the tortilla strips a few at a time in the remaining oil in a skillet over high heat until golden brown. Remove to paper towels to drain. Add tortilla strips and cheese to the soup; mix well. Garnish with sour cream, cheese and sliced avocado.

Italian Sausage Soup

6 tablespoons olive oil
1 cup chopped onions
4 large cloves of garlic, minced
6 (10-ounce) cans chicken or beef broth
1 cup chopped celery
3 carrots, peeled, sliced
1 (28-ounce) can peeled whole tomatoes with basil
1¹⁄₂ cups shredded cabbage
1 pound mild Italian sausage links
Salt and pepper to taste
Italian seasoning to taste
2 zucchini, sliced
3 to 4 ounces vermicelli, broken in half
3 tablespoons tomato paste
¹⁄₄ to ¹⁄₃ cup grated Parmesan cheese

Heat 3 tablespoons olive oil in a large saucepan over medium heat. Add the onions and 3 cloves of garlic. Sauté until golden brown. Add the broth, celery, carrots, tomatoes and cabbage; mix well. Place the sausages in a baking pan; prick each several times with a fork. Bake at 325 degrees until cooked through; drain. Slice the sausages. Add to the soup. Add the salt, pepper and Italian seasoning. Simmer until the vegetables are tender-crisp. Add the zucchini and vermicelli; mix well. Simmer until the vermicelli is tender. Heat the remaining olive oil in a small saucepan over medium heat. Sauté the remaining clove of garlic in the oil until golden brown. Add the tomato paste. Cook until the oil is absorbed into the tomato paste, stirring constantly. Add the Parmesan cheese; mix well. Stir the tomato mixture into the soup. Simmer the soup until heated through, stirring frequently.

Serves 8 to 10

Reuben Soup

Serves 6

6 slices German rye bread
3 quarts chicken broth
1 cup chopped cooked corned beef
2 cups chopped sauerkraut, drained
1/2 cup minced onion
1 teaspoon garlic powder
1/2 teaspoon white pepper
1 cup butter or margarine
1 cup flour
1 quart milk
8 ounces Swiss Almond Cheese, cubed

Combine the bread and broth in a large saucepan over medium heat. Simmer for 30 minutes or until bread is well broken up. Add the corned beef, sauerkraut, onion, garlic powder and pepper. Simmer for 20 minutes. Melt the butter in a medium saucepan over low heat. Add the flour. Cook for 5 minutes or until smooth, stirring constantly. Add the flour mixture to the soup. Cook until thickened, stirring occasionally. Add the milk and cheese. Simmer for 10 minutes, stirring occasionally. Serve with brown mustard, if desired.

Serves 16

Wild Raspberry Soup

Scott Tompkins
Marco Polo Café

4 cups wild raspberries
1 ripe peach, peeled and pitted
1/2 to 1 cup sugar
1/2 cup sour cream
Juice of 1/2 lemon

Combine the raspberries, peach and sugar in a blender container. Process until smooth. Add the sour cream and lemon juice. Process for 1 minute. Strain the soup into a bowl. Chill for 1 hour or until ready to serve.

Serves 4

If wild raspberries are not available, substitute fresh raspberries from the grocery store.

Cucumber Gazpacho

3 cups chicken broth
3 medium cucumbers, peeled, chopped
3 cups sour cream
3 tablespoons white vinegar
3 cloves of garlic, chopped
2 teaspoons salt
$^1/_2$ teaspoon white pepper

Combine the broth, cucumbers, sour cream, vinegar, garlic, salt and pepper in a blender container. Process until smooth, in batches if necessary. Transfer to a 2$^1/_2$-quart container. Chill for 4 hours. Garnish with at least 4 of the following: sautéed chopped almonds, chopped parsley, chopped tomatoes, chopped green onions, chopped green bell peppers, chopped black olives, chopped mushrooms or croutons.

Serves 8 to 10

Gazpacho Blanco

Roland Oberholzer
Roland's

1 rib celery, chopped
3 cucumbers, peeled, seeded, chopped
1 green bell pepper, seeded, chopped
$^1/_4$ cup chopped onion
$^1/_2$ teaspoon minced garlic
1 teaspoon freshly squeezed lemon juice
$^1/_2$ cup heavy cream (optional)
Salt and pepper to taste
Worcestershire sauce to taste
Hot pepper sauce to taste
1 cup chicken broth
2 cups sour cream

Combine the celery, cucumbers, green pepper, onion, garlic, lemon juice, cream, salt, pepper, Worcestershire sauce, pepper sauce and broth in a blender or food processor container. Process for 3 minutes or until smooth. Add the sour cream. Process until smooth. Chill for 1 hour. Garnish with fresh dillweed and chopped red bell peppers.

Serves 6

Summer Soup

12 fresh tomatoes
6 green onions, chopped
1 tablespoon salt
1 teaspoon sugar
1/2 teaspoon dried marjoram
1/2 teaspoon dried thyme
2 tablespoons freshly squeezed lime juice
2 teaspoons grated lime peel
1 1/2 cups sour cream
1 teaspoon curry powder

Peel and chop the tomatoes. Place in a blender container. Add the green onions, salt, sugar, marjoram, thyme, lime juice and lime peel. Process until the mixture is smooth. Add the sour cream and curry powder. Process until smooth. Chill for 1 hour. Serve garnished with chopped parsley.

Serves 4

Cold Tomato Bisque

1 tablespoon butter
1 cup chopped onion
2 cloves of garlic, minced
1 (28-ounce) can tomatoes
3/4 teaspoon dried dillweed
1 chicken bouillon cube
1/4 cup white wine
1/4 teaspoon salt
1/8 teaspoon pepper
1 cup nonfat plain yogurt
1/3 cup mayonnaise

Melt the butter in a saucepan over medium-high heat. Add the onion and garlic. Sauté for 5 minutes or until the onions are soft. Add the undrained tomatoes, dillweed, bouillon cube, wine, salt and pepper; mix well. Simmer for 15 minutes. Remove from the heat; let cool. Transfer the mixture to a blender or food processor container. Process until smooth, in batches if necessary. Transfer the mixture to a large bowl. Add the yogurt and mayonnaise; blend with a whisk until smooth. Chill, covered, for 1 hour.

Serves 8

Homemade croutons are delicious with this soup.

Sonoran Chicken Chili

1 tablespoon olive oil
1/2 cup chopped shallots
3 cloves of garlic, minced
2 (14-ounce) cans chopped tomatoes with
garlic, oregano and basil
1 (14-ounce) can whole tomatoes, chopped
1 (14-ounce) no-salt-added chicken broth
1 (4-ounce) can chopped green chiles
1/2 teaspoon oregano
1/2 teaspoon coriander
1/4 teaspoon cumin
4 cups chopped cooked chicken
1 or 2 (16-ounce) cans white beans, drained
3 tablespoons freshly squeezed lime juice
1/4 teaspoon pepper

Heat the olive oil in a large saucepan over medium-high heat. Add the shallots and garlic. Sauté until the shallots are soft. Add the seasonal tomatoes, undrained chopped tomatoes, broth, green chiles, oregano, coriander and cumin. Bring to a boil. Reduce the heat. Simmer for 20 minutes. Add the chicken and beans; mix well. Cook until heated through. Add the lime juice and pepper; mix well. Garnish with shredded Cheddar cheese.

Serves 8

Calico Chicken Chili

1 tablespoon butter
1 cup chopped onion
1 tablespoon ground cumin
4 boneless skinless chicken breasts,
cut into strips
1 (15-ounce) can white beans
1 (15-ounce) can chick-peas
2 (15-ounce) cans white corn, drained
2 (15-ounce) cans black beans, rinsed
1 (8-ounce) can chopped green chiles
3 cups water
3 chicken bouillon cubes

Heat the butter in a skillet over medium-high heat. Add the onion and cumin. Sauté until the onion is soft. Add the chicken. Sauté until cooked through. Transfer the mixture to a slow cooker or large stockpot. Add the white beans, chick-peas, corn, black beans, green chiles, water and bouillon cubes; mix well. Cook for 4 hours on High or simmer for 1 1/2 hours on the stove top. Garnish with chopped tomatoes, sour cream, chopped avocado, chopped cilantro, shredded cheese and tortilla chips.

Serves 6 to 8

Chasen's Chili

³/₄ pound pinto beans
5 cups chopped canned tomatoes
¹/₄ cup vegetable oil
1 green bell pepper, seeded, chopped
1 pound onions, chopped
2 cloves of garlic, crushed
¹/₂ cup chopped parsley
¹/₂ cup butter
2¹/₂ pounds lean ground beef
1 pound lean ground pork
1¹/₂ to 2 teaspoons chili powder
2 tablespoons salt
1¹/₂ teaspoons pepper
1¹/₂ teaspoons cumin seeds

Sort and rinse the beans. Place in a large saucepan, adding water to cover. Soak for 12 hours. Simmer, covered, over medium-low heat for 1¹/₂ hours or until tender. Add the tomatoes; mix well. Simmer for 5 minutes. Heat the oil in a large skillet over medium-high heat. Add the green pepper. Sauté for 5 minutes. Add the onions. Sauté until the onions are soft. Add the garlic and parsley; mix well. Remove from the heat; set aside. Melt the butter in a separate skillet over medium-high heat. Add the ground beef and ground pork, stirring until the meat is brown and crumbly; drain well. Add the meat to the onion mixture; mix well. Add the chili powder. Cook for 10 minutes. Add the meat mixture to the beans. Add the salt, pepper and cumin; mix well. Simmer, covered, for 1 hour. Remove the cover. Cook for 30 minutes. Skim and discard the fat from the top of the chili. Garnish with chopped onions and serve with crackers.

Serves 8

Chunky Chili

1/4 cup vegetable oil
2 cups chopped onions
4 cloves of garlic, minced
4 pounds stew beef, cubed
3 pounds spicy pork sausage
2 (28-ounce) cans whole tomatoes, chopped
1 (15-ounce) can tomato sauce
6 tablespoons chili powder
2 tablespoons cumin
2 tablespoons oregano
2 (16-ounce) cans baked beans
2 teaspoons salt
2 tablespoons sugar
1 tablespoon unsweetened baking cocoa
2 (15-ounce) cans red kidney beans
1 (15-ounce) can pinto beans
1 (4-ounce) can chopped green chiles

Heat the oil in a large Dutch oven over medium-high heat. Add the onions and garlic. Sauté until the onions are soft. Add the beef and sausage. Cook until the meat is brown and crumbly, stirring occasionally; drain well. Add the undrained tomatoes, tomato sauce, chili powder, cumin, oregano, baked beans, salt, sugar and cocoa; mix well. Simmer, partially covered, for 2 hours, stirring frequently. Add the kidney beans, pinto beans and green chiles; mix well. Simmer for 1 1/2 hours or until the beans are tender. Garnish with shredded cheese, sour cream, corn chips or sliced black olives.

Serves 16

A great dish to take on ski trips.

Green Chile Beef Stew

2 tablespoons lard or vegetable oil
2 pounds beef brisket, cubed
2 large onions, thinly sliced
1 clove of garlic, minced
1 (4-ounce) can chopped green chiles
1 (14-ounce) can plum tomatoes
1 cup chicken broth
1 avocado, peeled, pitted, chopped
8 ounces sour cream
2 limes, cut into wedges

Melt the lard in a Dutch oven over medium-high heat. Add the beef. Cook until brown on all sides. Transfer to a bowl; set aside. Add the onions and garlic to the drippings in the Dutch oven. Sauté until the onions are soft. Add the reserved beef, green chiles, undrained tomatoes and broth. Simmer, covered, for 2½ hours or until the meat is tender. Add the salt; mix well. Ladle stew into individual serving bowls. Top with avocado and sour cream. Squeeze fresh lime juice over the top. Serve immediately.

Serves 4 to 6

Wine Suggestion: Cotes du Rhone or Barbera

Breads & Brunch

Almond Poppy Seed Bread

3 eggs
1 1/2 cups milk
1 cup plus 2 tablespoons vegetable oil
2 1/4 cups sugar
2 tablespoons poppy seeds
1 1/2 teaspoons vanilla extract
1 1/2 teaspoons almond extract
1 1/2 teaspoons butter extract

3 cups sifted flour
1 1/2 teaspoons salt
1 1/2 teaspoons baking powder
1/4 cup orange juice
3/4 cup sugar
1 1/2 teaspoons vanilla extract
1 1/2 teaspoons almond extract
1 1/2 teaspoons butter extract

Combine the eggs, milk, oil and 2 1/4 cups sugar in a bowl; mix well with a fork. Add the poppy seeds, 1 1/2 teaspons vanilla, 1 1/2 teaspoons almond extract and 1 1/2 teaspoons butter extract; mix well. Add the flour, salt and baking powder. Beat by hand until well blended. Grease and flour two 8-inch loaf pans or 1 bundt pan. Pour the batter into the prepared pans. Bake at 350 degrees for 45 minutes or until a knife inserted in the center comes out clean. Cool for 10 minutes if in loaf pans or for 45 minutes if in a bundt pan. Combine the orange juice, 3/4 cup sugar, 1 1/2 teaspoons vanilla, 1 1/2 teaspoons almond extract and 1 1/2 teaspoons butter extract in a saucepan over medium heat. Cook until the sugar is dissolved, stirring constantly. Pour glaze over the warm bread.

Serves 10 to 12

Terrific as a holiday gift.

Luscious Cranberry Coffee Cake

1 teaspoon baking powder
1 teaspoon baking soda
2 cups sifted flour
$^1/_2$ teaspoon salt
$^1/_2$ cup butter or margarine, softened
1 cup sugar
2 eggs
1 cup sour cream
1 teaspoon almond extract
1 (7-ounce) can whole cranberry sauce
$^1/_2$ cup chopped pecans
$^3/_4$ cup confectioners' sugar
2 tablespoons hot water
$^1/_2$ teaspoon almond extract

Combine the baking powder, baking soda, flour and salt in a bowl; mix well. Cream the butter and sugar in a mixer bowl until light and fluffy. Add the eggs one at a time, beating well after each addition. Add the flour mixture alternately with the sour cream, beating well after each addition. Add 1 teaspoon almond extract; mix well. Grease and flour a bundt pan. Pour $^1/_3$ of the batter into the pan. Spread half the cranberry sauce over the batter carefully. Pour half the remaining batter over the cranberry sauce. Cover with remaining cranberry sauce. Cover with remaining batter. Sprinkle the top with chopped pecans. Bake at 325 degrees for 1 hour. Cool in the pan for 15 minutes. Remove coffee cake to a serving plate to cool completely. Combine the confectioners' sugar, water and $^1/_2$ teaspoon almond extract in a small bowl. Beat until smooth. Spread over coffee cake.

Serves 12

Raspberry Muffins with Streusel

Linda Hopkins
Les Petites Gourmettes

1¹/₂ cups flour
¹/₄ cup sugar
¹/₄ cup packed light brown sugar
2 teaspoons baking powder
¹/₄ teaspoon salt
1 teaspoon ground cinnamon
1 egg, beaten
¹/₂ cup melted butter
¹/₂ cup milk
1¹/₄ cups fresh raspberries
1 teaspoon grated lemon zest

¹/₂ cup chopped pecans
¹/₂ cup packed light brown sugar
¹/₄ cup flour
1 teaspoon ground cinnamon
1 teaspoon grated lemon zest
2 tablespoons melted butter
¹/₂ cup confectioners' sugar
1 tablespoon freshly squeezed lemon juice

Line 12 muffin cups with paper liners. Sift 1¹/₂ cups flour, sugar, ¹/₄ cup brown sugar, baking powder, salt and 1 teaspoon cinnamon together in a medium bowl. Make a well in the center. Place the egg, ¹/₂ cup butter and milk in the well. Stir with a wooden spoon just until combined. Stir in the raspberries and 1 teaspoon lemon zest. Fill the prepared muffin cups ³/₄ full. Mix the pecans, ¹/₂ cup brown sugar, ¹/₄ cup flour, 1 teaspoon cinnamon and 1 teaspoon lemon zest in a small bowl. Stir in 2 tablespoons butter. Sprinkle topping over each muffin. Bake at 350 degrees for 20 to 25 minutes or until a knife inserted in the center comes out clean. Remove to a wire rack to cool. Combine the confectioners' sugar and lemon juice in a bowl. Beat until smooth. Drizzle the glaze over the warm muffins.

Serves 12

Perfect for the child chef.

Almond French Toast

8 (^{1}/$_2$-inch-thick) slices French sourdough bread
3 ounces almond paste
3 ounces cream cheese, softened
4 eggs
^{1}/$_2$ cup milk
I teaspoon vanilla extract
3 tablespoons butter
I tablespoon vegetable oil

Remove the crusts from the bread. Place the crusts in a food processor container. Process until finely chopped. Remove the crumbs to a shallow dish; set aside. Place the almond paste and cream cheese in the food processor container. Process until smooth, scraping the side of the container as necessary. Combine the eggs, milk and vanilla in a shallow dish. Whisk until well mixed. Make 4 sandwiches using the almond mixture as the filling. Cut each sandwich diagonally to form 2 triangles. Heat the butter and oil in a large skillet over medium heat. Dip each triangle in the egg mixture, then the bread crumbs, then the egg mixture. Place in the skillet. Cook for 3 minutes on each side or until golden brown.

Serves 4

This is a family favorite and perfect for guests. Serve with preserves or with sour cream, whipped cream or warm pure maple syrup. It is also delicious served with sliced apples that have been sautéed in butter and sugar until slightly caramelized.

Autumn Pumpkin Bread

1 (15-ounce) can pumpkin purée
1¹/2 cups packed light brown sugar
1/2 cup melted butter or margarine
3 eggs, beaten
5 cups sifted flour
2 tablespoons baking powder
1 teaspoon cinnamon
1/2 teaspoon nutmeg
1/2 teaspoon salt
2 cups chopped walnuts

Coat 2 loaf pans with nonstick cooking spray; set aside. Cream the pumpkin, brown sugar, butter and eggs in a mixer bowl until light and fluffy. Sift the flour, baking powder, cinnamon, nutmeg and salt into a large mixer bowl. Make a well in the center. Add the creamed mixture; stir just until moistened. Fold in the walnuts gently. Spoon into the prepared pans. Bake at 350 degrees for 1 hour or until a knife inserted in the center comes out clean.

Serves 16

This is easy enough to be the children's contribution to a holiday dinner.

Irresistible Cheese Bread

1¹/4 teaspoons dry yeast
2 tablespoons warm water
3/4 cup milk
3 tablespoons melted butter
1 egg
2 tablespoons sugar
3/4 teaspoon salt
2¹/2 cups (about) flour
8 ounces mozzarella cheese, cubed
8 ounces Muenster cheese, cubed
1 egg, beaten

Mix the yeast and water in a large bowl. Let stand for 5 minutes or until foamy. Stir the milk into the butter in a saucepan. Warm over low heat. Add to the yeast mixture. Add 1 egg, sugar, salt and 2 cups of the flour; mix well. Add enough additional flour to make a soft dough. Knead on a floured surface for 3 minutes or until smooth and elastic. Place in a greased bowl, turning to coat. Let rise, covered, in a warm place until doubled in bulk. Punch down the dough. Let rise, covered, for 1 hour or until doubled in bulk. Roll the dough into a 13x16-inch rectangle. Cover with the cheese. Fold the long side over to cover the cheese, sealing the edges. Place on a nonstick baking sheet. Pierce the dough all over with a fork. Brush with the beaten egg. Bake at 400 degrees for 20 minutes or until golden brown.

Serves 6 to 8

Sunrise Cheese Bread

2 eggs
2 cups milk
2 cups baking mix
1 teaspoon salt
1 (4-ounce) can chopped green chiles
2 cups shredded Monterey Jack cheese

Grease a 1½-quart glass baking dish or 2 loaf pans. Beat the eggs in a large mixer bowl until foamy. Add the milk, baking mix and salt; beat until well mixed. Add the green chiles and cheese; mix well. Pour into the prepared dish. Bake at 350 degrees for 50 minutes or until golden brown.

Serves 12

Buttery Cheesy Bread Bites

1 loaf dry unsliced sandwich bread
1½ cups butter
3 cups shredded Cheddar cheese
½ teaspoon Worcestershire sauce
½ teaspoon dry mustard
⅛ teaspoon salt
2 egg whites

Remove and discard the crusts from the bread. Cut the bread into 1-inch cubes; set aside. Melt the butter and cheese in the top of a double boiler, stirring occasionally. Add the Worcestershire sauce, dry mustard and salt; mix well. Beat in the egg whites. Remove from the heat. Dip each bread cube into the cheese mixture. Place on a baking sheet and freeze. Store frozen bread bites in a freezer bag until ready to bake. Place frozen bread bites on a nonstick baking sheet. Bake at 325 degrees for 10 to 15 minutes or until golden brown. Serve with soup or as an appetizer.

Serves 12 to 16

Dilly Bread

3 cups flour
1 tablespoon sugar
2 teaspoons instant minced onion
2 teaspoons dried dillweed
$^1/_4$ teaspoon baking soda
1 teaspoon salt
2 envelopes dry yeast
1 cup creamed cottage cheese
$^3/_4$ cup water
1 egg

Combine 1$^1/_2$ cups of the flour, sugar, onion, dillweed, baking soda, salt and yeast in a large mixer bowl. Combine the cottage cheese and water in a small saucepan over low heat. Heat to 110 degrees. Do not boil. Add the cottage cheese mixture and egg to the dry ingredients. Beat for 3 minutes on medium speed. Add the remaining flour a little at a time, mixing well after each addition. Let stand for 15 minutes. Grease a 1$^1/_2$-quart baking dish or 5x9-inch loaf pan. Place the dough in the prepared dish. Let rise, covered, until doubled in bulk. Bake at 350 degrees for 45 to 60 minutes or until a knife inserted in the center comes out clean. Cool before slicing.

Serves 8 to 10

Can add 2 tablespoons of butter to the cottage cheese and water if a richer flavor is desired.

Irish Soda Bread

1 quart buttermilk
$^1/_4$ teaspoon baking soda
7 cups flour
2 cups raisins
$^1/_2$ cup sugar
2 tablespoons caraway seeds
2$^1/_2$ tablespoons baking soda
2 teaspoons salt

Combine the buttermilk and $^1/_4$ teaspoon baking soda in a mixer bowl; mix well. Combine the flour, raisins, sugar, caraway seeds, 2$^1/_2$ tablespoons baking soda and salt in a separate mixer bowl; mix well. Add the buttermilk mixture to the dry ingredients; mix well. Grease and flour three 4x8-inch loaf pans. Split dough into 3 portions; place 1 in each pan. Bake at 375 degrees for 1$^1/_4$ hours or until a knife inserted in the center comes out clean. Cool loaves in pans for 15 minutes. Remove to wire racks to cool completely. Serve sliced with butter and jam.

Serves 24

A great hostess gift.

Green Chile Corn Bread

1 cup butter, softened
1 cup sugar
4 eggs
1 (4-ounce) can chopped green chiles
1 (16-ounce) can cream-style corn
1/2 cup shredded Monterey Jack cheese
1/2 cup shredded Cheddar cheese
1/4 teaspoon salt
1 cup flour
1 cup yellow cornmeal
4 teaspoons baking powder

Combine the butter, sugar, eggs, green chiles, corn, Monterey Jack cheese, Cheddar cheese and salt in a mixer bowl; mix well. Add the flour, cornmeal and baking powder; mix well. Grease a 9x11-inch baking pan. Pour the batter into the prepared pan. Place the pan in a preheated 350-degree oven. Reduce the temperature to 300 degrees. Bake for 1 hour or until a knife inserted in the center comes out clean.

Serves 10

Easy to make. Sweet and cheesy.

Mushroom Crust Quiche

2 tablespoons butter
1/4 teaspoon garlic powder
8 ounces mushrooms, chopped
1/2 cup saltine cracker crumbs
1 tablespoon butter
1/2 cup chopped green onions
1 1/2 cups shredded Swiss cheese
1 cup cottage cheese
3 eggs
1/4 teaspoon cayenne
1/4 teaspoon paprika (optional)

Grease a 9-inch pie pan; set aside. Melt 2 tablespoons butter in a skillet over medium-high heat. Add the garlic powder; mix well. Add the mushrooms. Sauté until mushrooms are tender and most of the liquid is absorbed. Add the cracker crumbs; mix well. Press the mixture over the bottom and up the side of the prepared pan. Melt 1 tablespoon butter in the same skillet used for the mushrooms. Add the green onions. Sauté until the green onions are soft. Spread over the mushroom crust. Sprinkle the Swiss cheese over the green onions. Combine the cottage cheese, eggs and cayenne in a blender container. Process until smooth. Pour over the Swiss cheese. Sprinkle with paprika. Bake at 350 degrees for 30 minutes or until a knife inserted in the center comes out clean. Let stand for 15 minutes before serving.

Serves 6

*This quiche is wonderful served with a medley of fresh fruit. For variety,
use Monterey Jack cheese with green chiles, diced ham with Cheddar cheese, or bacon bits and
sautéed onion slices with Jarlsberg cheese.*

Arizona Quiche

1 1/2 cups shredded Monterey Jack cheese
1 cup shredded mild Cheddar cheese
1 partially baked (9-inch) piecrust
1 (4-ounce) can chopped green chiles
1 cup half-and-half
3 eggs, beaten
1/4 teaspoon salt
1/8 teaspoon cumin

Spread the Monterey Jack cheese and half the Cheddar cheese evenly over the bottom of the piecrust. Scatter the green chiles over the cheese. Combine the half-and-half, eggs, salt and cumin in a mixer bowl; mix well. Pour over the cheese carefully. Sprinkle the remaining Cheddar cheese over the top. Bake at 325 degrees for 40 minutes or until a knife inserted in the center comes out clean.

Serves 6

Springtime Quiche

6 ounces lean cooked ham, chopped
1 unbaked (8-inch) pie shell
1/2 cup half-and-half
6 tablespoons milk
3 eggs
1/4 cup shredded Cheddar cheese
1/4 teaspoon salt
1/2 teaspoon white pepper
12 asparagus tips, cooked, drained

Sprinkle ham over the bottom of the pie shell; set aside. Combine the half-and-half, milk, eggs, cheese, salt and white pepper in a mixer bowl; mix well. Pour over the ham. Arrange the asparagus tips over the top. Place the quiche on a baking sheet. Bake at 400 degrees for 35 to 40 minutes or until a knife inserted in the center comes out clean. Serve immediately.

Serves 4 to 6

Spinach Mushroom Brunch Bake

1/2 cup unsalted butter
6 to 8 cups sliced fresh mushrooms
1/4 cup chopped sun-dried tomatoes
1/2 teaspoon thyme
2 tablespoons chopped fresh basil
1/4 cup chopped onion
1 pound fresh spinach,
blanched, drained
1/3 cup crumbled cooked bacon
8 ounces ricotta cheese

2/3 cup grated Parmesan cheese
12 croissants, sliced horizontally
1 cup shredded mozzarella cheese
6 eggs
2 cups milk
1/2 teaspoon pepper
1 teaspoon salt
1/4 teaspoon nutmeg
3 tablespoons melted butter

Melt 3 tablespoons of the 1/2 cup butter in a large skillet over medium-high heat. Sauté the mushrooms in the butter until tender. Add the tomatoes, thyme and basil; mix well. Transfer to a bowl; set aside. Melt the remaining 5 tablespoons butter in the skillet. Add the onion. Sauté until soft. Add the spinach, bacon, ricotta cheese and 1/3 cup of the Parmesan cheese; mix well. Place 1/3 of the croissant slices crust side down in a buttered 9x13-inch baking dish. Spread the onion mixture over the croissants. Top with another 1/3 of the croissants crust side down. Spread the mushroom mixture over the top. Sprinkle the mozzarella cheese over the mushroom mixture. Arrange the remaining croissants crust side up over the mozzarella cheese. Combine the eggs, milk, pepper, salt and nutmeg in a bowl; mix well. Pour over the croissants, making sure that all croissant pieces are moistened. Chill, covered, for 1 or 2 days. Sprinkle the remaining Parmesan cheese over the top. Drizzle with 3 tablespoons melted butter. Bake, uncovered, at 375 degrees for 45 minutes or until brown.

Serves 8 to 12

Remember, this dish must be made days ahead of time.

Triple Cheese Bake

5 cups soft bread cubes
3 tablespoons melted butter
1 1/2 cups shredded Swiss cheese
1/4 cup shredded Monterey Jack cheese
1 pound bacon, cooked, drained, crumbled
8 eggs
1 2/3 cups milk
1/4 cup white wine
2 green onions, minced
1 tablespoon prepared brown mustard
1/2 cup sour cream
1/2 cup grated Parmesan cheese

Arrange the bread cubes on the bottom of a greased 9x13-inch baking pan. Drizzle with butter. Sprinkle Swiss cheese, Monterey Jack cheese and bacon over the bread. Combine the eggs, milk, wine, green onions and mustard in a bowl; mix well. Pour over the bread. Chill, covered with foil, for 6 to 24 hours. Let stand, uncovered, for 30 minutes. Bake at 325 degrees for 1 hour or until a knife inserted in the center comes out clean. Combine the sour cream and Parmesan cheese in a bowl; mix well. Spread over the top of the baked mixture. Return to the oven. Bake for 10 minutes or until golden brown.

Serves 8

Outstanding brunch item and great on a buffet.

Bev's Green Chile Casserole

2 (4-ounce) cans whole green chiles
12 eggs, separated
1 teaspoon salt
16 ounces sour cream
4 cups shredded Monterey Jack cheese
4 cups shredded Cheddar cheese
Seasoned salt to taste

Rinse the green chiles; remove the seeds and membranes. Beat the egg whites in a mixer bowl until stiff peaks form. Combine the egg yolks, salt and sour cream in a bowl; mix well. Fold the egg whites into the egg yolk mixture gently. Spread 2 tablespoons of the egg mixture over the bottom of a 10x14-inch baking pan. Layer the green chiles, Monterey Jack cheese, Cheddar cheese and egg mixture in the pan, lightly sprinkling each egg mixture layer with seasoned salt. Make 3 layers, ending with the egg mixture. Bake at 350 degrees for 50 minutes. Cool for 10 minutes before serving. Serve with sausage and sweet rolls for a great brunch.

Serves 6

Sunday Sausage Soufflé

1 pound hot ground breakfast sausage
6 eggs, beaten
1 cup milk
¹/₂ cup sour cream
2 slices bread, cubed
1 cup shredded Cheddar cheese
1 (4-ounce) can chopped green chiles
Salt and pepper to taste

Brown the sausage in a skillet, stirring until crumbly; drain well. Combine the eggs, milk and sour cream in a mixer bowl. Beat until well mixed. Add the bread, cheese and green chiles; mix well. Fold in the sausage. Pour into an ungreased soufflé dish. Bake at 350 degrees for 45 minutes. Serve immediately.

Serves 4

Our Favorite Punch

6 bananas
1 (12-ounce) can frozen orange
juice concentrate
1 (6-ounce) can frozen lemon juice
1 (46-ounce) can pineapple juice
3 cups water
2 cups sugar
2 quarts lemon-lime soda, chilled

Place the bananas in a blender container. Process until mashed. Add the orange juice concentrate, lemon juice, pineapple juice, water and sugar. Process until smooth. Freeze the mixture for at least 24 hours. Remove from the freezer 1 hour before serving. Mix with lemon-lime soda in a punch bowl to serve.

Serves 30

This is a great base for a rum punch.

Salads

Chilled Asparagus Salad

Vincent Guerithault
Vincent's on Camelback

2 pounds fresh asparagus
1 quart water
1 tablespoon salt
1 small red bell pepper, seeded, chopped
1 small yellow bell pepper, seeded, chopped
1 tablespoon chopped fresh basil
2 tablespoons olive oil
3 tablespoons lemon juice
Salt and pepper to taste

Trim 2 inches from the stems of the asparagus. Peel if necessary. Combine the water and salt in a large saucepan over high heat. Bring to a boil. Plunge the asparagus into the boiling water. Cook for 5 to 8 minutes or until tender-crisp; drain. Chill until cooled completely. Combine the red pepper, yellow pepper, basil, olive oil, lemon juice, salt and pepper in a small bowl. Whisk until well mixed. Drizzle over the asparagus. Serve immediately.

Serves 4

Delicious and low-fat, too.

Mediterranean Stuffed Avocados

$^2/_3$ cup crumbled feta cheese
2 small fresh tomatoes, chopped
$^1/_4$ cup chopped red onion
2 tablespoons chopped fresh parsley
2 tablespoons olive oil
1 tablespoon balsamic vinegar or
red wine vinegar
1 tablespoon chopped fresh
oregano or cilantro
Salt and pepper to taste
Lettuce leaves
2 large avocados, halved, pitted

Combine the feta cheese, tomatoes, onion, parsley, olive oil, vinegar, oregano, salt and pepper in a small bowl; mix well. Arrange lettuce leaves on 4 plates. Place an avocado half on each plate. Spoon stuffing into each avocado. Serve immediately.

Serves 4

These make a great light lunch.

Oven-Roasted Beets with

Baby Field Greens and Goat Cheese Dressing

Patrick Ponce Poblete
Lon's at Hermosa Inn

12 fresh beets, golf-ball size or smaller
$^1/_2$ cup olive oil
Salt and pepper to taste
8 ounces goat cheese, broken into chunks
$^1/_4$ cup cider vinegar
2 cloves of garlic, puréed
$^1/_4$ cup (about) milk
2 tablespoons chopped fresh oregano
$^1/_2$ pound mesclun or mixed baby field greens
1 cup roasted walnut halves

Remove and discard the stems from the beets. Place 2 tablespoons of the olive oil and salt and pepper to taste in a large bowl. Add the beets; toss to coat. Transfer the beets to a baking pan. Cover with foil. Bake at 350 degrees for 2 hours. Remove to paper towels to cool slightly. Squeeze each beet in a paper towel to remove the outer skin. Cut the beets in half; set aside. For the dressing, whisk the salt, pepper, goat cheese, vinegar and garlic in a bowl until mixed. Add the remaining olive oil slowly, whisking constantly. Add milk until of the desired consistency. Toss the beets with $^1/_2$ of the oregano, salt and pepper. Toss the greens with the dressing, remaining oregano, salt and pepper. Arrange 6 beet halves on individual salad plates. Place salad in the center of each plate. Top with walnuts.

Serves 4

Salads

Roy's Kula Onion and Tomato Salad

Roy Yamaguchi
Roy's

I cup pancetta, chopped
I cup extra-virgin olive oil
2 teaspoons each minced garlic and shallots
I cup julienned fresh basil
I cup white balsamic vinegar
Salt and pepper to taste
6 large fresh tomatoes, cored
8 ounces mixed baby greens
3 large Maui onions, julienned
¹/₂ cup crumbled bleu cheese

Cook the first 4 ingredients in a large skillet over low heat for 10 minutes or until the pancetta is brown, stirring occasionally. Remove from the heat; cool slightly. Add the basil, vinegar, salt and pepper; mix well. Cut each tomato into 6 pieces. Arrange equal portions of greens and tomatoes on each of 6 plates. Combine the pancetta mixture and onions in a large skillet over low heat. Cook until the onions are soft. Spoon over the tomatoes. Top with bleu cheese. Serve immediately.

Serves 6

*Can substitute Vidalia or Walla Walla onions
for a Maui version.*

Broccoli Delight

Carol Ellis
Arcadia Farms

I pound fresh broccoli
I pound bacon, cooked, crumbled
¹/₄ cup chopped red onion
¹/₂ cup raisins
6 tablespoons crushed currants
6 tablespoons crushed peanuts
I cup mayonnaise
¹/₂ cup sugar
2 teaspoons vinegar

Trim and discard the dark green leaves from the broccoli stems. Cut the stems into ¹/₄-inch slices. Cut the broccoli florets into bite-size pieces. Combine the broccoli florets, broccoli stems, bacon, onion, raisins, currants and peanuts in a bowl; mix well. Whisk the mayonnaise, sugar and vinegar together in a small bowl. Pour the mayonnaise mixture over the broccoli 1 or 2 hours before serving; mix well.

Serves 6 to 8

Salads

French Green Bean Salad

2 (12-ounce) packages frozen French-style green beans
1/2 cup chopped red onion
1/2 cup crumbled feta cheese
1/2 cup chopped walnuts
1 tablespoon lemon juice
1 tablespoon white wine vinegar
1 teaspoon Dijon mustard
1/4 teaspoon dried basil
1/4 teaspoon sugar
1/4 teaspoon salt
1/4 teaspoon white pepper
1/3 cup extra-virgin olive oil

Cook the green beans according to the package directions until tender-crisp; drain. Plunge immediately into ice water; drain well. Combine the green beans, onion, feta cheese and walnuts in a bowl with a lid. Combine the lemon juice, wine vinegar, Dijon mustard, basil, sugar, salt and white pepper in a small bowl. Whisk until well mixed. Whisk in the olive oil slowly. Add the dressing to the green bean mixture. Chill for 1 hour before serving.

Serves 8

This salad makes a sophisticated picnic dish.

Salads

Colorful Black Bean Salad

2 (15-ounce) cans black beans, drained, rinsed
1 (11-ounce) can corn kernels, drained
1 medium red bell pepper, chopped
1 bunch green onions, chopped
$^1/_4$ cup chopped red onion
3 cloves of garlic, minced
2 teaspoons chopped fresh basil
$1^1/_2$ teaspoons salt
1 teaspoon sugar
1 teaspoon pepper
$^1/_3$ cup red wine vinegar
$^1/_4$ cup light olive oil
5 to 6 red or green bell peppers or tomatoes,
halved, seeded

Combine the black beans, corn, red pepper, green onions, red onion, garlic and basil in a bowl; mix well. Combine the salt, sugar, pepper, wine vinegar and olive oil in a small bowl. Whisk until well mixed. Pour over the black bean mixture; toss to mix well. Spoon into the bell peppers or tomatoes. Serve immediately.

Serves 10 to 12

Southwest Black Bean and

Wild Rice Salad

$1^1/_2$ cups cooked black beans
1 head each romaine and red leaf lettuce, torn
1 bunch green onions, chopped
1 cucumber, sliced
2 tomatoes, chopped
2 avocados, peeled, pitted, chopped
2 cups broken blue corn chips
1 cup shredded Cheddar cheese
1 cup shredded pepper Jack cheese
1 teaspoon chili powder
1 teaspoon each cumin and cayenne
1 teaspoon garlic powder
$^3/_4$ cup cooked wild rice
French dressing

Mix the black beans, romaine lettuce, leaf lettuce, green onions, cucumber, tomatoes, avocados, corn chips, Cheddar cheese and Jack cheese in a large bowl. Combine the chili powder, cumin, cayenne, garlic powder and wild rice in a bowl; mix well. Add to the black bean mixture; mix well. Add enough French dressing to coat the ingredients; mix well. Serve immediately.

Serves 10

This is a Phoenix favorite.

Salads

Oriental Wild Rice Salad

1/2 cup wild rice
2 cups beef bouillon
1 cup frozen peas or chopped broccoli
2 ribs celery, sliced diagonally
4 green onions, sliced
2 tablespoons red wine vinegar
1 tablespoon soy sauce
1 teaspoon sugar
1/4 cup vegetable oil
2 teaspoons toasted sesame oil
1/4 cup toasted slivered almonds

Place the rice in a saucepan over high heat. Cover with water by 1 inch. Bring to a boil; drain well. Add the bouillon. Simmer, covered, for 45 minutes or until all the liquid is absorbed. Cook the peas in boiling water in a saucepan until tender-crisp; drain. Combine the peas, celery and green onions in a bowl; mix well. Combine the wine vinegar, soy sauce, sugar, vegetable oil and sesame oil in a bowl. Whisk to mix well. Pour over the warm cooked rice. Let stand until cool. Combine the rice and vegetable mixtures in a bowl. Add the almonds; mix well. Chill until ready to serve. Serve in lettuce cups.

Serves 4

This is also wonderful served warm.

Artichoke Rice Salad

1 package chicken rice mix
1 or 2 (6-ounce) jars marinated artichoke hearts
4 green onions, chopped
1/2 green bell pepper, chopped
12 pimento-stuffed olives, sliced
1 (8-ounce) can water chestnuts, sliced
1/3 cup mayonnaise
3/4 teaspoon curry powder
Lemon juice to taste
Cashews

Prepare the chicken rice according to the package directions, without butter; cool. Chop the artichoke hearts; reserve half the liquid. Combine the rice, artichoke hearts, green onions, green pepper, olives and water chestnuts in a bowl; mix well. Mix the mayonnaise, curry powder, lemon juice and the reserved artichoke liquid in a bowl. Pour over the rice mixture; mix well. Add the cashews; mix well. Chill for 2 hours.

Serves 4 to 6

May add cooked chicken or shrimp for a main dish salad.

Razz's Couscous Salad

Erasmo Kamnitzer
Razz's Restaurant

1 cup water
1¹/₄ cups couscous
¹/₈ teaspoon salt
³/₄ cup chopped tomatoes
¹/₂ cup chopped onion
1 cup chopped green or
red bell pepper
¹/₂ cup chopped cilantro
1 tablespoon chopped parsley
1 cup toasted nuts

¹/₂ cup chopped cucumbers
6 tablespoons lime juice
¹/₄ cup olive oil
2 tablespoons sesame oil (optional)
Salt and pepper to taste
1 cup mixed citrus segments (orange,
grapefruit, lime)
2 tablespoons mixed edible flowers
1 sweet potato, julienned, crisp-fried
1 tablespoon honey

Bring the water to a boil in a saucepan over high heat. Add the couscous and salt. Cover and remove from the heat. Let stand for 5 minutes or until all the water has been absorbed. Fluff with a fork; let cool. Mix the couscous, tomatoes, onion, green pepper, cilantro, parsley, nuts and cucumbers in a bowl. Whisk the lime juice, olive oil and sesame oil in a small bowl until mixed. Pour over the couscous; mix well. Season with salt and pepper. Serve surrounded by citrus segments and topped with flowers and fried sweet potatoes. Drizzle honey over the citrus segments.

Serves 4

To simplify, substitute Terra brand snack chips for the sweet potato.

Salads

Summer Pasta Salad

1 clove of garlic, minced
1 1/2 cups fresh basil leaves
3/4 cup chopped parsley
2/3 cup red wine vinegar
2 tablespoons Dijon mustard
2 cups light olive oil or canola oil
Salt and pepper to taste
8 to 10 ounces fresh tortellini or farfalle
1 tablespoon light olive oil
1 red bell pepper, chopped
1/2 cup chopped red onion
1 green bell pepper, chopped
1 small jicama, peeled, chopped
2 cups chopped cooked chicken, ham or beef
2 cups chopped salami
2 cups pine nuts
2 cups grated fresh Parmesan cheese

Place the garlic and basil in a food processor container. Process until finely chopped. Add the parsley, wine vinegar, Dijon mustard, 2 cups olive oil, salt and pepper. Process until well mixed; set aside. Cook the tortellini according to the package directions; drain. Cool and place in a large mixer bowl. Toss with 1 tablespoon olive oil. Add the red pepper, onion, green pepper, jicama, chicken, salami and pine nuts; toss to mix well. Pour the dressing over the pasta mixture; toss to coat. Add the Parmesan cheese; mix well. Serve garnished with extra basil and Parmesan cheese.

Serves 8 to 10

Hearts of Palm with

Tangy Lemon Dressing

**2 to 3 heads Boston lettuce, torn
White part of 5 green onions, sliced
I (14-ounce) can hearts of palm, drained, sliced horizontally
2 cloves of garlic, minced
2 teaspoons sugar
Grated peel of I lemon
I teaspoon seasoned salt
$^1/_2$ teaspoon cracked pepper
$^1/_4$ teaspoon paprika
6 tablespoons freshly squeezed lemon juice
6 tablespoons sour cream**

Combine the lettuce, green onions and hearts of palm in a large bowl; mix well. For the dressing, combine the garlic, sugar, lemon peel, salt, pepper, paprika, lemon juice and sour cream in a bowl. Whisk until well mixed. Pour over the salad; toss to coat.

Serves 8

This is a salad men really love.

Salads

Ultimate Caesar Salad

1 red bell pepper
8 slices bacon, cooked, crumbled
1/2 cup crumbled feta cheese
2 heads romaine lettuce, torn
1/4 cup unsalted sunflower seed kernels
3 tablespoons crumbled bleu cheese
1 egg, beaten (optional)
1 egg yolk (optional)
3 tablespoons lemon juice
1 clove of garlic, minced
1 teaspoon Worcestershire sauce
Hot pepper sauce to taste
Salad Supreme seasoning to taste
1/4 cup olive oil
1/2 cup grated Parmesan cheese

Place the red pepper under the broiler for 10 minutes or until blackened on all sides. Remove to a paper bag. Let stand for 10 minutes. Peel, seed and coarsely chop the red pepper. Combine the red pepper, bacon, feta cheese, lettuce, sunflower seed kernels and bleu cheese in a bowl; toss to mix well. Beat the egg, egg yolk, lemon juice, garlic, Worcestershire sauce, pepper sauce and Salad Supreme seasoning in a bowl until well mixed. Add the olive oil gradually, beating constantly. Pour the dressing over the salad; toss to coat. Sprinkle the Parmesan cheese over all; toss to mix well. Serve immediately.

Serves 6

Brown Derby Cobb Salad with

Special French Dressing

1/2 head iceberg lettuce, chopped
1/2 bunch watercress, chopped
1 small bunch chicory, chopped
1/2 head romaine lettuce, chopped
2 tablespoons minced chives
2 medium tomatoes, peeled,
seeded, chopped
2 cups chopped cooked chicken
6 slices bacon, cooked, crumbled
1 avocado, peeled, pitted, chopped
3 hard-cooked eggs, chopped
1/2 cup crumbled Roquefort cheese

1/4 cup water
1/4 cup red wine vinegar
1/4 teaspoon sugar
1 1/2 teaspoons lemon juice
1/2 teaspoon salt
1/2 teaspoon pepper
1/2 teaspoon Worcestershire sauce
3/4 teaspoon Coleman's dry mustard
1/2 clove of garlic, minced
1/4 cup olive oil
3/4 cup vegetable oil

Combine the iceberg lettuce, watercress, chicory, romaine lettuce and chives in a large bowl; toss to mix well. Arrange the tomatoes, chicken, bacon, avocado and eggs over the lettuces. Sprinkle the Roquefort cheese over the top. Chill for 1 hour. For the dressing, combine the water, wine vinegar, sugar, lemon juice, salt, pepper, Worcestershire sauce, mustard, garlic, olive oil and vegetable oil in a bowl. Whisk until well mixed. Chill until ready to serve. Pour 1/2 cup of the dressing over the salad; toss to coat. Serve immediately. Store the remaining dressing, covered, in the refrigerator.

Serves 8 to 10

Always terrific.

Salads

Marge's Mexican Salad

I head lettuce, torn
¹/₂ cup shredded Cheddar or
Monterey Jack cheese
¹/₂ cup chopped green onions
¹/₂ cup chopped black olives
4 medium tomatoes, sliced
I avocado, peeled, pitted, mashed
I tablespoon lemon juice
¹/₂ cup sour cream
¹/₃ cup vegetable oil
¹/₂ teaspoon sugar
¹/₂ teaspoon garlic salt
¹/₂ teaspoon chili powder
I cup crushed tortilla or corn chips

Combine the lettuce, cheese, green onions, black olives and tomatoes in a bowl; toss to mix well. Combine the avocado, lemon juice, sour cream, oil, sugar, garlic salt and chili powder in a blender container. Process until smooth. Pour over the salad; toss to mix well. Stir in corn chips just before serving.

Serves 4

Spinach Salad with

Chutney Dressing

I pound fresh spinach
6 mushrooms, sliced
I cup sliced water chestnuts
6 slices bacon, cooked, crumbled
³/₄ cup fresh bean sprouts
¹/₂ cup shredded Gruyère cheese
¹/₄ cup sliced red onion
¹/₄ cup wine vinegar
2 tablespoons chopped Major Grey's chutney
I clove of garlic, minced
2 tablespoons French mustard
2 teaspoons sugar
¹/₂ cup vegetable oil
Salt and pepper to taste

Wash, dry and tear the spinach into bite-size pieces. Combine the spinach, mushrooms, water chestnuts, bacon, bean sprouts, Gruyère cheese and onion in a large bowl. For the dressing, combine the wine vinegar, chutney, garlic, mustard, sugar, oil, salt and pepper in a small bowl. Whisk until well mixed. Pour over the salad; toss to coat. Serve immediately.

Serves 4 to 6

Add cold sliced pork tenderloin for a main dish salad.

Salad Primavera with

Citrus Caper Dressing

1 orange
1 cup chopped watercress
6 cups torn romaine lettuce
1 (9-ounce) package frozen artichoke
hearts, thawed, drained, chopped
$^1/_2$ cup chopped red bell pepper
$^1/_4$ cup chopped green onions
$^1/_3$ cup orange juice
$^1/_4$ cup white wine vinegar

2 tablespoons chopped fresh parsley
2 tablespoons Dijon mustard
$^1/_4$ teaspoon olive oil
1 tablespoon minced capers
1 teaspoon sugar
1 teaspoon minced garlic
$^1/_4$ teaspoon freshly ground pepper
2 tablespoons freshly grated
Parmesan cheese to taste

Peel the orange. Separate into sections and cut each section in half. Combine the orange pieces, watercress, romaine lettuce, artichoke hearts, red pepper and green onions in a bowl; toss to mix well. For the dressing, combine the orange juice, wine vinegar, parsley, Dijon mustard, olive oil, capers, sugar, garlic and pepper in a jar with a tight-fitting lid. Shake until well mixed. Chill until ready to serve. Shake well before using. Pour the dressing over the salad; toss to mix well. Sprinkle Parmesan cheese over the top just before serving.

Serves 8

The Citrus Caper Dressing complements seafood entrées nicely.

Salads

Spinach Garden Vegetable Salad

2/3 cup plain yogurt
1/3 cup mayonnaise
2 teaspoons Dijon mustard
3 green onions, thinly sliced
2 cloves of garlic, minced
6 cups fresh spinach leaves
2 1/2 cups sliced mushrooms
2 medium carrots, thinly sliced
1 cup halved cherry tomatoes
2 cups alfalfa or mixed sprouts
1/2 medium cucumber, thinly sliced
1/2 red or green bell pepper, chopped
1/4 cup roasted sunflower seed kernels

Combine the yogurt, mayonnaise and Dijon mustard in a bowl; mix until smooth. Add the green onions and garlic; mix well. Chill, covered, for 1 hour to blend the flavors. Combine the spinach, mushrooms, carrots, tomatoes, sprouts, cucumber and red pepper in a large bowl; toss to combine. Pour the dressing over the salad; toss to coat. Sprinkle with sunflower seed kernels.

Serves 6

Radish roses make a beautiful garnish for this salad.

Fruit and Spinach Salad

8 slices bacon
1/2 cup sliced almonds
10 cups spinach, torn
1 small Pippin apple, cored, chopped
1 small Red Delicious apple, cored, chopped
1 small pear, cored, chopped
4 green onions, sliced
1 teaspoon honey
1/4 cup vegetable oil
3 tablespoons raspberry vinegar
1/2 teaspoon mustard
Salt and pepper to taste

Brown the bacon in a skillet over medium-high heat. Remove to paper towels to drain; crumble and set aside. Add the almonds to the drippings in the skillet. Sauté until the almonds are brown. Remove to paper towels to drain. Combine the bacon, almonds, spinach, apples, pear and green onions in a large bowl. Add the honey; toss to coat. Combine the oil, vinegar, mustard, salt and pepper in a bowl. Whisk until well mixed. Pour the dressing over the salad; toss to coat.

Serves 8

A crunchy and delicious combination.

Salads

Mandarin Salad with

Raspberry Vinaigrette

1 head romaine or green leaf lettuce, torn
1 small jicama, peeled, julienned
2 (10-ounce) cans mandarin oranges, drained
1 avocado, peeled, pitted, sliced
$^2/_3$ cup toasted slivered almonds
1 (12-ounce) can frozen raspberry-cranberry concentrate
1 (16-ounce) jar seedless raspberry jam
2 teaspoons minced garlic
$^1/_2$ teaspoon salt
1 teaspoon white pepper
2 cups red wine vinegar
4 cups safflower oil

Combine the lettuce, jicama, oranges, avocado and almonds in a large bowl; toss to mix. Combine the raspberry-cranberry concentrate, jam, garlic, salt and pepper in a blender container. Process until smooth. Add the wine vinegar. Process for 1 to 2 minutes. Add the safflower oil slowly with the blender running. Process until smooth. Add desired amount of dressing to the salad; toss to coat.

Serves 6 to 8

Salads

Strawberry Salad

1 (3-ounce) package strawberry gelatin
³/4 cup boiling water
1 (12-ounce) package frozen sliced
strawberries, thawed
1 banana, mashed
1 (8-ounce) can crushed pineapple
1 cup sour cream

Place the gelatin in a bowl. Pour the boiling water over the gelatin, stirring until the gelatin is dissolved. Add the strawberries, banana and undrained pineapple; mix well. Pour ¹/2 of the mixture into a salad mold. Chill until set. Add the sour cream to the remaining gelatin mixture; mix well. Pour over the molded gelatin. Chill until firm.

Serves 10

Pear and Bleu Cheese Salad

**Scott Tompkins
Marco Polo Café**

¹/2 cup canola oil
3 tablespoons corn syrup
2 tablespoons rice wine vinegar
1¹/2 teaspoons Dijon mustard
5 ounces crumbled bleu cheese
4 red pears, cut into eighths
4 green pears, cut into eighths
Salad greens

Combine the canola oil, corn syrup, wine vinegar and Dijon mustard in a bowl; mix well. Add the bleu cheese; mix well. Cover and chill until serving time. Arrange the pears over the salad greens. Stir the dressing and pour over the pears.

Serves 10

Salads

Salmon Mousse with

Cucumber Sauce

1 (10-ounce) can tomato soup
8 ounces cream cheese, softened
2 envelopes unflavored gelatin
$^1/_2$ cup cold water
1 cup mayonnaise
1 (15-ounce) can salmon, drained,
or 2 cups poached fresh salmon
1 cup chopped celery
$^1/_2$ cup chopped green bell pepper
$^1/_2$ cup chopped onion
2 tablespoons minced parsley
2 drops of hot pepper sauce
$^1/_4$ teaspoon marjoram

$^1/_4$ teaspoon thyme
$^1/_8$ teaspoon tarragon
Salt and pepper to taste
1 cup sour cream or yogurt
1 cucumber, peeled, seeded, minced
2 tablespoons dillweed
1 tablespoon minced onion
1 teaspoon prepared mustard
1 teaspoon salt
$^1/_8$ teaspoon garlic powder
2 tablespoons freshly squeezed
lemon juice

Place the soup and cream cheese in the top of a double boiler. Heat until the cream cheese melts, stirring occasionally. Soften the gelatin in the cold water. Add to the soup mixture. Stir until the gelatin dissolves. Remove from the heat. Cool to lukewarm. Add the mayonnaise, salmon, celery, green pepper, chopped onion, parsley, pepper sauce, marjoram, thyme, tarragon, salt and pepper to taste; mix well. Pour the salmon mixture into a greased 2-quart mold. Chill for 6 hours or overnight. For the sauce, combine the sour cream, cucumber, dillweed, minced onion, mustard, 1 teaspoon salt, garlic powder and lemon juice in a bowl; mix well. Chill until ready to serve. Unmold salmon mousse onto a bed of lettuce and garnish with parsley. Serve the sauce on the side.

Serves 8

Salads

Smoked Salmon Cheesecake with

Watercress Salad

Robert McGrath
The Roaring Fork

2 cups Ritz cracker crumbs
6 tablespoons melted unsalted butter
2 cups cream cheese, softened
2 tablespoons cornstarch
2 eggs, beaten
³/4 cup heavy cream
1 cup chopped smoked salmon
2 tablespoons chopped chives

Kosher salt and pepper to taste
¹/4 cup champagne vinegar
2 tablespoons extra-virgin olive oil
2 tablespoons chopped fresh dillweed
6 ounces smoked salmon slices
2 tablespoons Topiko caviar
2 bunches watercress

Combine the cracker crumbs and melted butter in a bowl; mix well. Press the mixture over the bottom and 1 inch up the side of a 9¹/2-inch springform pan. Bake at 350 degrees for 5 minutes. Remove to a wire rack to cool completely. Increase the oven temperature to 425 degrees. Beat the cream cheese and cornstarch in a mixer bowl until light and fluffy. Add the eggs; beat until well mixed. Add the cream and salmon gradually; mix well. Fold in the chives, salt and pepper. Pour into the prepared crust. Bake for 30 minutes or until the filling is set around the edges. Remove to a wire rack to cool completely. Chill for 2 hours or overnight. For the dressing, mix the vinegar, olive oil, dillweed, salt and pepper in a bowl. Arrange a slice of cheesecake off-center on a plate. Arrange smoked salmon slices over the cheesecake. Top with a dollop of caviar. Place the watercress next to the cheesecake. Drizzle the dressing over the watercress.

Serves 4

Salads

Sonoran Barbecued Shrimp Salad

Rick Sederholt
Remington's Restaurant at The Scottsdale Plaza Resort

1 cup prickly pear syrup
1/4 cup balsamic vinegar
3 tablespoons minced fresh basil
1/2 cup olive oil
2 tablespoons mixed
southwestern spices
2 cloves of garlic, minced
20 large shrimp, peeled, deveined
8 slices carrot
8 slices red onion
8 slices eggplant
3 tablespoons olive oil

Salt and pepper to taste
1/4 cup balsamic vinegar
1 clove of garlic, minced
2 tablespoons minced fresh basil
1 teaspoon herbes de Provence
1/2 cup olive oil
1 tablespoon Dijon mustard
1 teaspoon minced fresh oregano
8 cups assorted mixed salad greens
4 plum tomatoes quartered
1/2 cup toasted pine nuts

Mix the pear syrup, 1/4 cup vinegar, 3 tablespoons basil, 1/2 cup olive oil, southwestern spices and 2 cloves of garlic in a nonreactive bowl. Add the shrimp. Marinate in the refrigerator for 2 hours. Brush the carrot, onion and eggplant slices with 3 tablespoons olive oil. Season with salt and pepper. Grill vegetables over hot coals for 3 minutes on each side. Remove from the heat. Place 5 shrimp on each of four 10-inch bamboo skewers. Cook over hot coals for 4 minutes on each side or until cooked through, brushing frequently with the marinade. For the dressing, combine 1/4 cup vinegar, 1 clove of garlic, 2 tablespoons basil, herbes de Provence, 1/2 cup olive oil, Dijon mustard, oregano, salt and pepper in a bowl. Whisk until well mixed. Combine the salad greens, tomatoes, grilled vegetables and desired amount of dressing in a bowl; toss to mix. Arrange the salad on each of 4 chilled plates. Remove the shrimp from the skewers. Arrange the shrimp over the salad. Sprinkle with pine nuts. Serve with warm tortillas.

Serves 4

Salads

Smoked Salmon Potato Salad

Scott Tompkins
Marco Polo Café

1 tablespoon Dijon mustard
1 tablespoon chopped fresh dillweed
3 tablespoons olive oil
1/3 cup orange juice
2 tablespoons orange zest
Salt and pepper to taste
8 cooked small red potatoes, sliced
4 ounces smoked salmon, chopped
1/2 red onion, julienned
1 tablespoon capers, rinsed

Combine the Dijon mustard, dillweed, olive oil, orange juice, orange zest, salt and pepper in a bowl; mix well. Cover and chill thoroughly. Combine the potatoes, salmon, onion and capers in a bowl; toss to mix well. Pour the dressing over the potato mixture and toss to mix well.

Serves 4

Easy and impressive.

Seafood Vermicelli Salad

1 to 2 pounds shrimp or crab meat, cooked
2 cups lemon juice
1 rib celery, chopped
1 red onion, chopped
1 white onion, chopped
1 pound vermicelli, cooked, drained
1 cup mayonnaise
Pepper to taste
1 teaspoon celery seeds, or to taste

Combine the shimp and lemon juice in a non-reactive bowl; mix well. Marinate in the refrigerator for 2 to 3 hours. Combine the celery, red onion, white onion, vermicelli and drained shrimp in a bowl; mix well. Add the mayonnaise; toss to coat well. Add the pepper and celery seeds; mix well. Chill for 12 hours.

Serves 12

Salads

Charred Beef Salad

James McDevitt
Restaurant Hapa

1 teaspoon pepper	1 serrano chile, seeded, minced
1/4 cup soy sauce	1 cup julienned seeded cucumber
1/4 cup sugar	1 cup julienned seeded ripe papaya
1 teaspoon minced garlic	1/4 cup julienned fresh mint
1/4 cup oyster sauce	1/4 cup thinly sliced red onion
8 ounces filet mignon, cut into	1/4 cup freshly squeezed lime juice
2 ounce pieces	Salt and pepper to taste
2 cups julienned green papaya	2 cups canola oil
1 plum tomato, seeded, julienned	1/2 cup rice stick noodles

Combine 1 teaspoon pepper, soy sauce, sugar, garlic and oyster sauce in a shallow bowl; mix well. Remove and reserve 1/2 cup of the soy sauce mixture. Add the beef to the remaining mixture. Marinate in the refrigerator for 3 to 6 hours. Combine the green papaya, tomato, serrano chile, cucumber, ripe papaya, mint and onion in a large bowl; toss to mix well. Add the lime juice, salt and pepper; toss to mix well. Chill for 1 hour. Heat the canola oil in a deep saucepan over medium-high heat. Separate the rice stick noodles. Add them to the hot oil in small batches. Cook for 10 to 15 seconds. Remove to paper towels to drain. Drain and discard the marinade from the beef. Place a large nonstick skillet over high heat. Add the beef. Cook for 1 minute on each side or to desired degree of doneness. Remove the beef to a plate; set aside. Remove the papaya mixture from the refrigerator; toss lightly. Cut the beef into thin slices. Add to the papaya mixture. Place a mound of the beef mixture on each of 4 plates. Drizzle with the reserved soy sauce mixture. Top with crispy rice stick noodles.

Serves 4

Suggested wine: Kings Estate Pinot Gris, Oregon or Beringer Pinot Noir

Salads

Asian Chicken Salad

$^1/_3$ **cup mayonnaise**
1 $^1/_2$ **tablespoons freshly squeezed lemon juice**
2 teaspoons soy sauce
$^1/_2$ **teaspoon sesame oil**
1 drop of hot pepper sauce
1 $^1/_2$ **cups chopped cooked chicken breast**
$^1/_3$ **cup thinly sliced green onions**
$^1/_2$ **cup chopped lightly toasted walnuts**
Salt and pepper to taste

Combine the mayonnaise, lemon juice, soy sauce, sesame oil and pepper sauce in a bowl. Whisk to mix well. Add the chicken, green onions, walnuts and salt and pepper; toss to combine.

Serves 3 to 4

You can serve this as a salad in a red cabbage leaf or as a sandwich on 12-grain wheat bread with snow peas.

Spicy Oriental Chicken Salad

2 cups water
1 (3-inch) piece fresh ginger, peeled
4 boneless skinless chicken breasts
¹/₄ cup soy sauce
2 tablespoons dry sherry
4 teaspoons sesame oil
¹/₄ teaspoon red pepper flakes
2 teaspoons sugar
¹/₄ cup each chopped scallions and cilantro
2 cups chopped water chestnuts

Bring water and ginger to a boil in a saucepan. Simmer, covered, for 15 minutes. Remove ginger to a plate to cool. Chop enough ginger for 1 teaspoon. Return the water to a boil. Add the chicken. Reduce heat to low. Cook, covered, for 15 minutes or until cooked through. Remove the chicken to a plate to cool. Combine the soy sauce, sherry, sesame oil, red pepper, sugar, scallions, cilantro and water chestnuts in a bowl; mix well. Add the chopped ginger; mix well. Shred the chicken. Add to the soy sauce mixture; toss to mix. Chill for 30 minutes. Serve on a bed of Bibb lettuce.

Serves 4 to 6

This salad is also great as an appetizer with double the amount of red pepper flakes and served on endive lettuce leaf tips.

Japanese Chicken Salad

4 boneless skinless chicken breasts
1 head lettuce, or 1 bunch fresh spinach
1 bunch green onions, chopped
¹/₂ cup slivered almonds
3 tablespoons sugar
3 tablespoons poppy seeds
2 teaspoons salt
¹/₂ teaspoon pepper
¹/₄ cup cider vinegar
¹/₂ cup vegetable oil
1 small can Chinese noodles

Grill or broil the chicken. Cool and cut the meat into bite-size pieces. Tear the lettuce into bite-size pieces. Combine the chicken, lettuce, green onions and almonds in a large bowl; toss to mix well. Combine the sugar, poppy seeds, salt, pepper, vinegar and oil in a bowl. Whisk to mix well. Pour the dressing over the chicken mixture; toss to coat. Sprinkle noodles over the top of the salad just before serving.

Serves 4 to 5

Salads

Irresistible Chicken Salad

4 cups shredded cooked chicken
3 cups seedless grapes, halved
2 cups chopped celery
1 cup mayonnaise
1/2 cup sour cream
1 teaspoon ground ginger
1 tablespoon sugar
1 teaspoon salt
2 tablespoons grated lemon peel
2 tablespoons lemon juice

Combine the chicken, grapes and celery in a large bowl; mix well. Combine the mayonnaise, sour cream, ginger, sugar, salt, lemon zest and lemon juice in a small bowl. Whisk until well mixed. Pour over the chicken mixture; mix well. Chill, covered, to blend the flavors. Serve over lettuce.

Serves 8

A great light and refreshing summer salad.

Buffalo Chicken Salad

1 1/2 teaspoons paprika
2 tablespoons vegetable oil
2 teaspoons hot pepper sauce
8 boneless skinless chicken breasts
3/4 cup shredded carrots
1/2 cup chopped celery
6 cups torn romaine lettuce
2 cups cherry tomatoes, quartered

Combine the paprika, oil and pepper sauce in a nonreactive bowl. Add the chicken breast halves, turning to coat well. Marinate, covered, in the refrigerator for 1 hour or overnight. Combine the carrots, celery, lettuce and tomatoes in a bowl; mix well. Chill, covered, for 1 hour. Drain the chicken, discarding the marinade. Place the chicken on a grill rack sprayed with oil. Grill the chicken over hot coals for 4 to 5 minutes on each side or until cooked through. Remove from the grill and cut diagonally across the grain. Arrange the lettuce mixture on 8 plates. Arrange chicken slices in a fan over the lettuce. Serve with your favorite bleu cheese dressing.

Serves 8

A salad twist on a favorite appetizer.

Hawaiian Chicken Salad

6 cups chopped cooked chicken
1 cup sliced celery
1 bunch green onions, chopped
1 cup cashews
1 (11-ounce) can pineapple tidbits
4 ounces sour cream
1/2 cup mayonnaise
1 teaspoon curry powder
2 teaspoons freshly squeezed lime juice
1/3 cup chopped Major Grey's chutney

Combine the chicken, celery, green onions and cashews in a bowl; mix well. Drain the pineapple; reserve the juice. Add the pineapple to the chicken mixture; mix well. Combine the reserved pineapple juice, sour cream, mayonnaise, curry powder, lime juice and chutney in a bowl; mix well. Pour over the chicken mixture; toss to coat. Serve in a hollowed-out pineapple half.

Serves 8

Oriental Slaw

¹/₂ head green cabbage, shredded
3 green onions, sliced
3 tablespoons toasted slivered almonds
3 tablespoons toasted sesame seeds
1 (4-ounce) can sliced water chestnuts
1 package chicken-flavored ramen
noodles, crumbled
¹/₃ cup rice wine vinegar
1 cup vegetable oil
¹/₄ teaspoon garlic powder
1 teaspoon sugar
Ground pepper to taste

Combine the cabbage, green onions, almonds,
sesame seeds and water chestnuts in a bowl; mix
well. Sprinkle the seasoning packet from the ramen
noodles over the top. Add the noodles; mix well.
Combine the wine vinegar, oil, garlic powder, sugar
and pepper in a bowl. Whisk until well mixed. Pour
over the cabbage mixture; toss to coat.

Serves 4

*Add warm grilled chicken breasts to make this
a summer luncheon salad.*

Cool Bleu Dressing

Mark Tarbell
Tarbell's

6 to 8 tablespoons freshly squeezed lemon juice
Sea salt to taste
1 to 3 cloves of garlic, minced
¹/₂ cup nonfat mayonnaise
¹/₈ teaspoon Worcestershire sauce
2 tablespoons extra-virgin olive oil
5¹/₂ ounces crumbled bleu cheese
¹/₄ cup grated Parmesan or Romano cheese

Combine the lemon juice, sea salt, garlic, mayonnaise
and Worcestershire sauce in a bowl. Whisk to mix
well. Add the oil gradually, whisking after each
addition. Add the bleu cheese and Parmesan cheese;
mix well. Serve over iceberg lettuce wedges.

Serves 6

Entrées

Beef Grand Marnier

1 (2- to 4-pound) beef tenderloin
1 cup Grand Marnier
1 cup barbecue sauce
2 teaspoons minced garlic
2 teaspoons minced onion
Salt and pepper to taste
8 ounces sliced Monterey Jack cheese

Make a $^1/_4$-inch-deep slit across the length of the tenderloin. Place the tenderloin in an ungreased loaf pan. Pour the Grand Marnier and barbecue sauce over the tenderloin. Scatter the garlic, onion, salt and pepper over the top. Chill, covered, for 4 to 6 hours. Place the loaf pan over hot coals in a grill; cover. Grill for 45 minutes or until done to taste. Arrange the cheese slices over the top of the tenderloin. Grill until the cheese is melted. Slice and serve.

Serves 6 to 8

Wine suggestion: California Cabernet Sauvignon, or Syrah, Australian Cabernet Sauvignon, or Shiraz

Great for casual grilling.

Preston's Chateaubriand

1 cup chablis
1 (4- to 6-pound) beef tenderloin
$^1/_2$ cup butter
$^1/_2$ cup cognac
$^1/_4$ teaspoon thyme
$^1/_2$ bay leaf
$^1/_2$ cup chopped onion (optional)
1 pound mushrooms, sliced

Pour the chablis in a large shallow dish. Place the tenderloin in the wine; turn to coat. Marinate, covered, in the refrigerator for 12 hours. Melt the butter in a saucepan over medium-high heat. Add the cognac, thyme, bay leaf and onion. Simmer until the mixture is reduced by half. Add the mushrooms. Simmer for 3 to 4 minutes. Remove the tenderloin from the marinade. Cut a pocket in the tenderloin. Stuff the mushroom mixture into the pocket. Tie the tenderloin securely or use small skewers to seal the pocket. Grill the tenderloin on a spit over hot coals until done to taste, basting often with the marinade. May roast in a 375-degree oven for 45 minutes or until done to taste, basting often with the marinade.

Serves 4 to 6

Wine suggestion: Pomerol, Merlot, Red Burgundy (should be at least 6 years old)

Teriyaki Beef Tenderloin

1/2 cup dry sherry
1/4 cup soy sauce
2 tablespoons dry onion soup mix
2 tablespoons packed light brown sugar
2 to 2 1/2 pounds beef tenderloin
2 tablespoons water

3 tablespoons prepared
horseradish sauce
1 tablespoon prepared mustard
1/2 teaspoon seasoned salt
1 cup sour cream

Combine the sherry, soy sauce, soup mix and brown sugar in a large, sealable plastic bag. Seal and press the bag to mix the contents. Place the tenderloin in the bag. Turn to coat with the marinade. Place the bag in a deep bowl to steady the meat. Marinate for 2 hours at room temperature or overnight in the refrigerator. Turn the bag several times to coat the meat with marinade. Remove the tenderloin to a rack placed in a shallow roasting pan. Roast at 425 degrees for 1 hour or until a meat thermometer registers 160 degrees, basting occasionally with half the marinade. Place the remaining marinade in a saucepan over medium-high heat. Bring to a boil. Remove the tenderloin to a cutting board. Cut into 1/4-inch slices. Arrange the slices on a serving platter. Cover with the hot marinade. Garnish with watercress. Combine the horseradish, mustard, salt and sour cream in a mixer bowl. Beat on medium speed until well mixed. Chill, covered, until ready to serve. Serve the tenderloin with horseradish sauce on the side.

Serves 6 to 8

Wine suggestion: Zinfandel, Australian Shiraz

Entrées

Beach-Style Carne Asada

1 (14-ounce) can tomatoes
1 (4-ounce) can chopped green chiles
1 bunch green onions, chopped
3 tablespoons vegetable oil
1 tablespoon vinegar
1 tablespoon leaf oregano
1 to 2 sprigs of cilantro
1 teaspoon ground oregano
1 teaspoon coriander
1/2 teaspoon onion salt or garlic salt
1 (1 1/2- to 2-pound) flank steak
8 small flour tortillas, warmed

Mash the tomatoes in a bowl. Add the green chiles, green onions, oil, vinegar, dried leaf oregano and cilantro; mix well. Chill the salsa for several hours to blend the flavors. Combine the ground oregano, coriander and onion salt in a small bowl; mix well. Rub the mixture into both sides of the steak. Place the steak on a grill over hot coals. Grill for 7 minutes on each side or until done to taste. Do not overcook. Remove to a cutting board. Cut across the grain into 1/2-inch strips. Place a few strips on each flour tortilla. Top with salsa. Fold each tortilla to enclose the steak.

Serves 4

Wine suggestion: Shiraz, or serve Mexican beer

Reuben Casserole

1 (28-ounce) can sauerkraut, drained, rinsed
2 medium tomatoes, sliced
2 tablespoons Thousand Island salad dressing
2 tablespoons butter
8 ounces shredded corned beef
2 cups shredded Swiss cheese
1 (10-count) can flaky biscuits
2 crisp rye crackers, crushed
1/4 teaspoon caraway seeds

Layer the sauerkraut, tomatoes, salad dressing, butter, corned beef and cheese in an 8x12-inch baking dish. Bake at 425 degrees for 15 minutes. Separate each biscuit into 3 layers. Arrange the biscuit layers over the beef mixture in 3 rows, overlapping the biscuits. Sprinkle cracker crumbs and caraway seeds over the biscuits. Bake for 15 to 20 minutes or until the top is brown.

Serves 8

Wine Suggestion: Alsatian Riesling, or serve German beer

A hearty one-dish family meal.

Entrées

Amazing-But-True Lasagna

3 (16-ounce) cartons low-fat ricotta cheese or cottage cheese
2 eggs, beaten
16 ounces grated Parmesan cheese
Salt to taste
1 teaspoon garlic powder, or to taste
1 teaspoon oregano, or to taste
3 (26-ounce) jars prepared or homemade spaghetti sauce
2 (16-ounce) packages lasagna noodles, uncooked
2 (16-ounce) packages shredded mozzarella cheese

Combine ricotta cheese, eggs, half the Parmesan cheese, salt, garlic powder and oregano in a bowl; mix well. Spread 1 cup of the spaghetti sauce in the bottom of a 9x13-inch baking pan. Alternate layers of uncooked noodles, ricotta mixture, spaghetti sauce and mozzarella cheese until all are used. Sprinkle the remaining Parmesan cheese over the top. Chill, covered, for 12 hours. Bake at 350 degrees for 1 hour or until golden brown and bubbly. Let stand for 10 minutes before cutting and serving.

Serves 12 to 14

Wine suggestion: Dolcetto Barbera, Chianti Classico, California Sangiovese

Entrées

Lasagna Classico

1/2 cup chopped onion
1 pound lean ground beef, or 1 pound bulk
sausage and 1/2 pound ground beef
2 tablespoons olive oil
2 cloves of garlic, minced
1/4 teaspoon pepper
1 teaspoon garlic salt
1 1/2 teaspoons dried oregano, or to taste
3 tablespoons chopped parsley, or to taste
1 (28-ounce) can Italian tomatoes
1 (8-ounce) can tomato sauce
2 tablespoons grated Parmesan cheese
1/2 teaspoon fennel seeds (optional)
1/2 to 3/4 (1-pound) package lasagna noodles
1 pound mozzarella cheese, thinly sliced
16 ounces ricotta cheese
8 ounces cottage cheese
1 cup grated Parmesan cheese, or to taste

Sauté onion and meat in olive oil in skillet over medium-high heat until meat is brown and crumbly, stirring often; drain. Add the next 9 ingredients. Simmer for 30 minutes. Cook noodles using package directions. Alternate layers of sauce, noodles and cheeses in a 8x12-inch baking dish, making 3 layers of each. Bake at 350 degrees for 30 minutes or until brown and bubbly.

Serves 8 to 10

Wine suggestion: Chianti Classico

Mexican Lasagna

2 pounds ground chuck
1 green bell pepper, seeded, chopped
1 cup chopped onion
2 tablespoons chili powder
1 tablespoon (heaping) minced garlic
2 teaspoons salt
1 tablespoon pepper
2 cups white sauce
2 (4-ounce) cans chopped green chiles
12 small corn tortillas, cut into strips
4 cups shredded Monterey Jack cheese, or
Cheddar cheese

Cook the ground beef with the green pepper and onion in a skillet over medium-high heat until the ground beef is brown and crumbly; drain. Add the chili powder, garlic, salt and pepper; mix well. Add the white sauce and green chiles; mix well. Spread a layer of the ground beef mixture over the bottom of a 9x13-inch baking dish. Add a layer of tortilla strips, a layer of meat and a layer of cheese. Continue layering until all ingredients are used, ending with cheese. Bake at 325 degrees for 50 minutes. Serve with sour cream and guacamole on the side.

Serves 8 to 10

Wine suggestion: serve Mexican beer

Entrées

Barbecued Leg of Lamb with

Ginger and Cilantro

1 tablespoon coriander seeds
1/4 cup chopped onion
1/2 cup chopped cilantro
1 (1-inch) piece fresh ginger, peeled, chopped
6 cloves of garlic, halved
1 teaspoon black peppercorns, crushed
2 tablespoons sea salt
1/2 cup strained freshly squeezed lemon juice

1/4 cup olive oil
1 (7-pound) leg of lamb, boned, separated into 3 pieces
3 large tomatoes, cored, chopped
1 cup dry white wine
3 tablespoons Dijon mustard
Kosher salt to taste
pepper to taste
1/2 cup butter, cut into small pieces
2 tablespoons chopped cilantro

Cook the coriander seeds in a dry skillet over medium-high heat until lightly toasted. Crush the seeds. Combine the seeds and next 8 ingredients in a glass dish; mix well. Chill the lamb in the marinade for 2 days, turning once or twice. Drain the lamb. Reserve the marinade. Bring the tomatoes and wine to a boil in a saucepan over medium-high heat. Simmer over low heat for 20 minutes or until thickened. Add 1/4 cup of the reserved marinade; mix well. Cook for 2 minutes. Strain the mixture through a strainer into a heatproof bowl, pressing to extract liquid. Add the Dijon mustard to the liquid; mix well. Add kosher salt and pepper; mix well. Place the bowl over boiling water. Add the butter a little at a time, beating well after each addition. Add 2 tablespoons cilantro; mix well. Boil the remaining reserved marinade in a saucepan over high heat for 2 minutes; cool. Pat the lamb dry. Grill over hot coals for 10 minutes on each side, basting frequently with the remaining marinade and turning once. Roll the lamb in the remaining marinade. Let stand for 5 minutes before slicing. Serve with the wine sauce.

Serves 8 to 10

Wine suggestion: Australian Shiraz, Côte-Rotie, Zinfandel

Entrées

Oriental Leg of Lamb

¹/₃ cup hoisin sauce
3 tablespoons rice wine vinegar
2 tablespoons soy sauce
2 tablespoons minced garlic
¹/₃ cup minced green onions
1 tablespoon honey
¹/₂ teaspoon salt
1 (4¹/₂- to 5¹/₂-pound) boneless butterflied
leg of lamb, trimmed

Combine the hoisin sauce, wine vinegar, soy sauce, garlic, green onions, honey and salt in a bowl; whisk until well mixed. Place the lamb in a shallow dish. Pour the hoisin mixture over the lamb; turn to coat all sides. Marinate in the refrigerator for 4 hours or overnight, turning at least once. Remove the lamb from the refrigerator. Bring to room temperature. Place the lamb on an oiled grill rack 5 to 6 inches above hot coals. Grill for 12 to 15 minutes per side or until a meat thermometer inserted in the thickest part registers 140 degrees. Remove to a cutting board. Let stand for 15 minutes before carving.

Serves 4 to 6

Wine suggestion: Zinfandel, Châteauneuf-du-Pape,
Australian Shiraz

Easy and Elegant

Rack of Lamb

1 (8- to 9-rib) rack of lamb, trimmed, frenched
Salt and freshly cracked black pepper to taste
¹/₄ cup extra-virgin olive oil
1 large shallot, minced
1 clove of garlic, minced
¹/₈ teaspoon red pepper flakes
2 tablespoons minced fresh rosemary
¹/₂ cup dry bread crumbs

Rub the lamb with salt and pepper. Brown in 2 tablespoons of the olive oil in a skillet over medium-high heat. Remove to a shallow roasting pan. Add the remaining oil to the skillet. Add the shallot. Sauté for 5 minutes or until soft. Add the garlic, red pepper flakes and rosemary. Cook for 1 minute, stirring occasionally. Remove from heat. Add the bread crumbs; mix well. Press the crumb mixture onto all exposed surfaces of the lamb. Roast at 475 degrees for 15 minutes or until a meat thermometer registers 130 degrees for medium-rare. Let stand for 10 minutes. Slice between ribs.

Serves 4

Wine suggestion: Red Bordeaux (at least 10 years old),
Cabernet Sauvignon

Double-Cut Pork Chops with Apple Cinnamon au Jus

Eddie Matney
Eddie Matney's Epicurian Trio

4 (10-ounce) pork chops, frenched
1/2 cup orange juice
1/4 cup pineapple juice
1/2 teaspoon baking soda
1/2 teaspoon dark rum
1/8 teaspoon red pepper flakes
Salt and pepper to taste
1 tablespoon olive oil
3 large sweet potatoes, baked
1/2 cup butter
2 tablespoons honey
2 tablespoons heavy cream
1/8 teaspoon ginger
2 cups unfiltered apple cider
1 clove of garlic, minced
1 shallot, minced
1 stick cinnamon
2 tablespoons brandy
1 tablespoon honey
1 teaspoon chopped habanero
1/2 teaspoon salt
1/4 teaspoon pepper
1 tablespoon cornstarch
1 tablespoon apple cider

Marinate pork chops in the next 5 ingredients in a sealable plastic bag for 6 hours.
Drain; pat dry. Sprinkle with salt and pepper. Cook in oil in a skillet over medium-high
heat until brown on both sides. Remove to a baking pan. Bake at 400 degrees for 10
minutes or until cooked through. Mash unpeeled sweet potatoes, next 4 ingredients and
salt and pepper to taste in a bowl. Combine the next 9 ingredients in a saucepan over
high heat. Simmer for 10 minutes or until reduced by 1/4, stirring occasionally. Add
cornstarch dissolved in 1 tablespoon cider. Cook until thickened, stirring constantly.
Serve each pork chop with 1 cup of the sweet potatoes. Ladle the sauce over all.

Serves 4

Wine suggestion: Gigondas, Zinfandel, Australian Shiraz

Entrées

Chinese Pork Tenderloins

1 cup Major Grey's chutney, finely chopped
2 tablespoons white vinegar
2 tablespoons sugar
2¹/2 cups plum jelly or preserves
¹/4 teaspoon minced fresh ginger
3 cloves of garlic, minced
10 tablespoons sugar
4 teaspoons dark molasses
1 cup soy sauce
1 teaspoon salt
2 teaspoons prepared hot mustard
2 to 4 pork tenderloins
¹/4 cup dry mustard
1 teaspoon vinegar
Water

Combine the chutney, white vinegar, sugar, jelly and ginger in a bowl; mix well. Combine ¹/4 cup of the chutney mixture, garlic, sugar, molasses, soy sauce, salt and prepared mustard in a bowl; mix well. Place the pork in a large sealable plastic bag. Pour the marinade mixture over the pork, turning to coat. Marinate, covered, in the refrigerator for 3 to 4 hours or overnight. Remove the pork from the marinade. Boil the marinade in a small saucepan over high heat for 1 minute. Bake the pork at 300 degrees for 1 hour or until cooked through, basting occasionally with the reserved marinade. Combine the dry mustard and vinegar in a small bowl; mix well. Stir in enough water to make a smooth paste. Serve the tenderloin thinly sliced with the mustard sauce and the remaining chutney mixture.

Serves 6 to 8

Wine suggestion: Zinfandel, Côtes du Rhône

Entrées

Pork Tenderloin with

Mustard Sauce

1 (1-pound) pork tenderloin
1/4 cup soy sauce
1/4 cup bourbon
2 tablespoons packed brown sugar
1/3 cup sour cream
1/3 cup mayonnaise
1 tablespoon dry mustard
1 tablespoon chopped green onion
1/2 teaspoon vinegar
Salt to taste

Marinate the pork in a mixture of the soy sauce, bourbon and brown sugar in a sealable plastic bag in the refrigerator for 1 hour. Remove the pork. Boil the marinade in a saucepan over high heat for 1 minute. Bake the pork at 325 degrees for 1 hour, basting often with the marinade. Combine the sour cream, mayonnaise, mustard, green onion, vinegar and salt in a small bowl; mix well. Serve the pork sliced with the mustard sauce on the side.

Serves 3 to 4

Wine suggestion: Zinfandel, Syrah

Great with Pacific Wave Rice (page 152).

Waikiki Ribs

4 to 5 pounds baby back pork loin ribs
Seasoned salt to taste
1 cup soy sauce
1 cup honey
1 cup catsup
3 tablespoons grated fresh gingerroot
2 cloves of garlic, minced
1/2 teaspoon pepper

Parboil the ribs in boiling water for 30 minutes; drain. Cut into individual ribs. Rub each rib with seasoned salt. Combine the soy sauce, honey, catsup, gingerroot, garlic and pepper in a sealable plastic bag; mix well. Add the ribs, turning to coat on all sides. Marinate in the refrigerator for 12 hours. Remove the ribs to a baking pan, arranging in a single layer. Glaze each rib with additional honey. Bake at 350 degrees for 30 minutes or until cooked through and tender.

Serves 4 to 6

Wine suggestion: Gigondas, Zinfandel

This may also be served as an appetizer.

Committee's Chalupas

3 pounds boneless pork loin or butt
2 cloves of garlic, minced
1 teaspoon oregano
1 tablespoon plus 1 teaspoon ground cumin
1 teaspoon salt
1 (16-ounce) can tomatoes
2 (14-ounce) cans chicken broth
1/2 cup chopped onion
2 (7-ounce) cans chopped green chiles
1 pound dry pinto beans, rinsed
1/4 teaspoon red pepper flakes
6 quarts (about) water

Trim and discard the excess fat from the pork.
Combine the pork, garlic, oregano, cumin, salt,
tomatoes, broth, onion, green chiles, beans and red
pepper flakes in a large saucepan or soup pot. Add
water. Bring to a boil. Reduce the heat. Simmer,
covered, for 3 to 6 hours, stirring often. Add more
water as needed. Shred the pork into bite-size
pieces. Serve over tostado chips. Garnish with
shredded cheese, chopped onions, sour cream,
guacamole, chopped tomatoes, shredded lettuce,
salsa or black olives.

Serves 12 to 16

Wine suggestion: Sangría, or serve Mexican beer

Piccata con Carciofi

1/4 cup flour
1/2 teaspoon salt
1/2 teaspoon pepper
1/2 teaspoon basil
1/2 teaspoon oregano
2 pounds veal or chicken, sliced for scallopini
2 large cloves of garlic, minced
2 tablespoons olive oil
2 tablespoons butter
1 package frozen artichoke hearts,
cooked, halved
1/2 pound mushrooms, sliced, sautéed in butter
1 cup chicken broth
1/4 cup freshly squeezed lemon juice

Combine the first 5 ingredients in a bowl; mix well.
Coat the meat with the flour mixture; set aside.
Sauté the garlic in the olive oil and butter in a skillet
over medium-high heat for 30 seconds. Add the
meat. Sauté until cooked through, turning once. Add
the artichoke hearts and mushrooms; mix well. Add
the broth. Bring to a boil. Reduce heat. Simmer,
covered, for 15 minutes. Add the lemon juice; mix
well. Remove to a heated platter. Garnish with
capers, lemon slices and parsley.

Serves 4 to 6

*Wine suggestion: Bordeaux Blanc, Australian
Sémillon Pinot Grigio*

Entrées

Veal Chops with

Cognac Cream Sauce

4 double-thick veal chops, at room temperature
Salt and freshly cracked pepper to taste
3 tablespoons unsalted butter
I large shallot, minced
I cup chicken broth
$^1/_4$ cup cognac
$^1/_2$ cup heavy cream

Season the veal chops with salt and pepper. Melt the butter in a large skillet over medium-high heat. Add the veal chops. Cook for 5 minutes on each side or until brown. Add the shallot. Sauté for 5 minutes or until the shallot is soft and light brown. Add half the chicken broth; mix well. Reduce the heat. Simmer, covered, for 6 minutes. Remove the veal chops to a plate; keep warm. Remove the skillet from the heat. Add the cognac; mix well. Add the remaining chicken broth. Place over high heat. Bring to a boil. Cook until the mixture is reduced to $^1/_2$ cup. Add the cream. Reduce the heat. Simmer until the mixture thickens, stirring often. Serve the veal chops with the cream sauce.

Serves 4

Wine suggestion: White Burgundy, California Chardonnay, Light St. Émilion

Artichoke Chicken Casserole

1 (24-ounce) jar marinated artichokes,
drained, quartered
2 cups cooked rice
4 cups shredded cooked chicken breast
2 (10-ounce) cans cream of chicken soup
^{1}/2 cup milk
1 cup mayonnaise
1 teaspoon lemon juice
^{1}/2 teaspoon curry powder
1^1/4 cups shredded sharp Cheddar cheese
^{1}/2 pound mushrooms, sliced
^{3}/4 cup seasoned bread crumbs, or equal parts
Parmesan cheese and bread crumbs
2 tablespoons butter

Arrange the artichokes in a 9x13-inch baking pan. Add a layer of the rice and chicken. Combine the next 5 ingredients, ^{3}/4 cup of the cheese and mushrooms in a bowl; mix well. Pour over the chicken. Sprinkle the remaining cheese over the top. Sauté the bread crumbs in the butter in a skillet over medium-high heat until light brown, stirring constantly. Spread the crumbs over the cheese. Bake at 350 degrees for 30 minutes. May be made the night before and chilled until ready to bake. Prepare and add the bread crumbs just before baking.

Serves 8 to 10

Wine suggestion: Bordeaux Blanc, Sauvignon Blanc

Chicken Breasts with

Roasted Garlic Sauce

Donna Nordin
Café Terra Cotta

1 bulb of garlic
1 tablespoon olive oil
2 tablespoons butter
3 cups heavy cream
4 ounces goat cheese, softened
Salt and white pepper to taste
6 boned chicken breasts, cooked

Brush the garlic bulb with olive oil. Wrap in foil. Bake at 200 degrees for 2 hours; cool. Squeeze out the cloves. Cook in the butter in a skillet until a smooth paste forms, stirring constantly. Simmer the cream in a saucepan over medium-high heat until reduced by half. Add the reduced cream and goat cheese to the garlic mixture. Simmer until smooth, stirring constantly. Season with salt and white pepper. Serve the chicken with the garlic sauce.

Serves 6

Wine suggestion: Hermitage Blanc, California Chardonnay, Côtes du Rhône Blanc

Entrées

Chicken Phyllo Casserole

4 boneless skinless chicken breasts,
cut into 1-inch cubes
1/4 cup unsalted butter
1/3 cup Dijon mustard
2 tablespoons minced fresh tarragon, or
2/3 teaspoon dried
1 1/2 cups heavy cream
1 tablespoon dry sherry
2 tablespoons Worcestershire sauce

Salt and white pepper to taste
1/4 cup chopped onion
5 mushrooms, sliced
1/4 cup unsalted butter
1 red bell pepper, julienned
1 green bell pepper, julienned
3/4 cup melted unsalted butter
10 sheets phyllo pastry

Sauté the chicken in 1/4 cup butter in a large skillet over medium-high heat for 5 minutes or until cooked through. Remove to a shallow bowl; keep warm. Add the Dijon mustard and tarragon to the skillet; mix well. Cook until reduced slightly, stirring often. Reduce heat to low. Add the cream. Cook until reduced by 1/4, stirring often. Add the sherry and Worcestershire sauce; mix well. Pour over the chicken; toss to coat. Season with salt and white pepper. Sauté the onion and mushrooms in 1/4 cup butter in a skillet over medium-high heat until the onion is soft; drain and discard any liquid. Add the bell peppers. Sauté until heated through but still crisp. Brush 1 tablespoon of the melted butter over the bottom and sides of a medium baking dish. Place 1 sheet of pastry over the butter, allowing the pastry to hang over the edges of the pan. Pat the pastry into the corners and sides of the pan. Repeat the process 4 times, brushing each sheet of pastry with butter. Pour the chicken mixture into the pan. Layer the pepper mixture on top. Layer 5 more sheets of pastry over the peppers, brushing each sheet with butter. Trim the excess pastry to 1 inch from the edge of the pan. Fold the edges of the pastry toward the center of the pan, brushing thoroughly with butter to keep the pastry in place. Bake at 350 degrees for 25 minutes or until golden brown.

Serves 8

Wine suggestion: dry Sauvignon Blanc, Pouilly Fumé

Entrées

Creamy Calvados Chicken

2 tablespoons butter
1 tablespoon vegetable oil
4 large tart apples, cored, cut into ¹/₄-inch slices
2 teaspoons cinnamon, divided
2 tablespoons butter
1 tablespoon vegetable oil
8 boneless skinless chicken breasts
2 white or Vidalia onions, sliced
1 cup Calvados, dry sherry or apple juice
¹/₂ cup heavy cream or concentrated chicken broth
1 teaspoon salt
1 teaspoon white pepper

Heat 2 tablespoons butter and 1 tablespoon oil in a skillet over medium heat. Add the apples and 1 teaspoon cinnamon. Sauté for 2 minutes or until tender-crisp; remove to a plate and keep warm. Add 2 tablespoons butter and 1 tablespoon oil to the skillet. Brown the chicken over high heat for 5 minutes on each side or until golden brown. Remove to a plate and keep warm. Add the onions to the drippings in the skillet. Cook until golden brown, stirring occasionally. Add the Calvados. Sauté for 1 minute. Return the chicken to the pan. Simmer, covered, until the chicken is cooked through. Arrange the chicken on a serving platter. Add the cream, 1 teaspoon cinnamon, salt and white pepper to the drippings in the skillet. Bring to a boil. Cook until the sauce is reduced by ¹/₃, stirring often. Arrange the apple slices on top of the chicken. Pour the sauce over all. Garnish with a sprinkling of cinnamon.

Serves 6 to 8

Wine suggestion: Alsatian Gewürztraminer, Riesling, Rhinegau Riesling

An astonishing apple entrée.

Crusty Chicken with

Chunky Italian Salsa

4 boneless chicken breasts
Salt and pepper to taste
2 eggs, beaten
1¹/₂ cups fresh bread crumbs
¹/₂ cup grated Parmesan cheese
1¹/₂ teaspoons grated lemon peel
2 bunches arugula, trimmed, chopped
4 plum tomatoes, seeded, chopped
6 tablespoons olive oil
¹/₄ cup chopped red onion
2 tablespoons chopped fresh basil
1 tablespoon balsamic vinegar
1 tablespoon freshly squeezed lemon juice

Season the chicken with salt and pepper. Coat with the egg. Coat with a mixture of the bread crumbs, Parmesan cheese and lemon peel. Combine the arugula, tomatoes, 2 tablespoons of the olive oil, onion, basil, vinegar, lemon juice, salt and pepper in a bowl; mix well. Brown the chicken in the remaining oil in a skillet over medium-high heat for 5 minutes per side or until cooked through. Remove to a serving platter; top with the salsa.

Serves 4

Wine suggestion: Pinot Grigio

Cumberland Chicken

¹/₂ cup grated Parmesan cheese
2 cups seasoned bread crumbs
3 tablespoons sesame seeds
4 whole chicken breasts, split
¹/₂ cup melted butter
1 cup red currant jelly
1 (6-ounce) can frozen orange juice
concentrate, thawed
¹/₄ cup wine or sherry
1 teaspoon dry mustard
¹/₈ teaspoon ginger
¹/₄ teaspoon hot pepper sauce

Combine the Parmesan cheese, bread crumbs and sesame seeds in a shallow dish. Dip each chicken piece in the butter. Dip in the crumb mixture. Place in a shallow baking pan. Drizzle any remaining butter over the chicken. Bake at 350 degrees for 30 to 45 minutes or until the chicken is cooked through. Combine the jelly, orange juice concentrate, wine, dry mustard, ginger and pepper sauce in a saucepan; mix well. Simmer over medium heat until smooth, stirring frequently. Serve with the chicken.

Serves 8

*Wine suggestion: California Cabernet Franc,
Bandol, Merlot*

Great for those too busy to cook.

Grilled Margarita Chicken

²/₃ cup olive oil
¹/₂ cup freshly squeezed lime juice
¹/₄ cup tequila
¹/₈ cup triple sec
¹/₄ cup chopped fresh cilantro
4 boneless skinless chicken breasts

Combine the olive oil, lime juice, tequila, triple sec and cilantro in a nonreactive bowl; mix well. Add the chicken; turning to coat. Marinate, chilled, for 4 hours, turning once. Remove the chicken from the marinade. Pour the marinade into a saucepan over high heat. Boil for 1 minute. Grill the chicken over hot coals for 10 to 15 minutes or until cooked through, turning 3 or 4 times. Baste liberally with the marinade.

Serves 4

Wine suggestion: Vouvray, dry Chenin Blanc

Scrumptious summer selection.

Lemon Cream Chicken

4 boneless skinless chicken breasts, pounded
Salt and pepper to taste
6 tablespoons butter
2 tablespoons freshly squeezed lemon juice
2 tablespoons grated lemon peel
2 tablespoons sherry or dry vermouth
2 tablespoons butter
1 cup heavy cream
2 tablespoons butter
2 tablespoons grated Parmesan cheese

Sprinkle the chicken with salt and pepper. Melt 6 tablespoons butter in a skillet over medium-high heat. Sauté the chicken for 5 to 8 minutes or until cooked through, turning once. Remove the chicken to an ovenproof platter. Add the lemon juice, lemon peel, sherry and 2 tablespoons butter to the skillet. Reduce the heat. Add the cream. Cook until thickened, whisking constantly. Pour the mixture over the chicken. Dot with 2 tablespoons butter. Sprinkle with Parmesan cheese. Place under the broiler. Broil until brown. Serve extra sauce over the chicken.

Serves 4

Wine suggestion: Australian Sémillon, Bordeaux Blanc, Chardonnay

Pasta with Maple Mustard Chicken

Linda Hopkins
Les Petites Gourmettes

2 large cloves of garlic, minced
2 tablespoons olive oil
2 tablespoons chopped fresh rosemary
2 tablespoons chopped fresh chives
2 tablespoons apple cider vinegar
$^1/_3$ cup pure maple syrup
$^1/_4$ cup spicy brown mustard
6 boneless skinless chicken breasts
Salt to taste
Pepper to taste

1 tablespoon olive oil
1 cup white wine
1 cup chicken broth
3 red bell peppers, roasted, peeled, seeded, chopped
$^1/_2$ cup sun-dried tomatoes, chopped
$^1/_2$ pound snow peas, stemmed, lightly steamed
1 pound penne pasta, cooked

Sauté the garlic in 2 tablespoons olive oil in a large skillet over medium heat for 30 seconds. Add the rosemary, chives and vinegar. Cook for 30 seconds, stirring constantly. Transfer to a bowl; cool. Whisk in the syrup and mustard. Sprinkle the chicken with pepper. Marinate, chilled, in a glass dish for 1 hour or overnight. Remove the chicken from the marinade, reserving the marinade. Season with salt and pepper. Sauté in 1 tablespoon olive oil in a large skillet over medium-high heat for 2 minutes per side. Reduce heat to medium. Cook for 3 minutes per side or until cooked through. Remove chicken to a cutting board. Add the wine to the skillet. Bring to a boil. Cook until reduced by $^1/_2$. Add the chicken broth and reserved marinade. Boil for 5 minutes or until reduced to desired consistency. Cut the chicken into bite-size cubes. Add the chicken, red peppers, tomatoes and snow peas to the sauce. Cook until heated through. Season with salt and pepper. Combine chicken mixture and pasta in a bowl; mix well.

Serves 8

Wine suggestion: California Sangiovese, Vouvray

Entrées

Santa Fe Kiev

¹/₄ cup butter
1 tablespoon minced onion
1 clove of garlic, minced
2 Anaheim chiles, cut into strips, chopped
2 ounces goat cheese, softened
2 ounces cream cheese, softened
4 boneless skinless chicken breasts
1 cup sour cream
1 (4-ounce) can chopped green chiles

Melt the butter in a skillet over medium-high heat. Add the onion, garlic and Anaheim chiles. Sauté until the onion is soft; set aside. Combine the goat cheese and cream cheese in a small bowl; mix well and set aside. Pound the chicken breasts between 2 sheets of plastic wrap until flattened. Spread ¹/₄ of the vegetables over each chicken breast. Place 1 tablespoon of the cheese mixture in the middle of each chicken breast. Roll tightly to enclose the cheese completely. Secure with wooden picks. Chill, covered, for 8 to 24 hours. Place the chicken in a baking pan. Bake at 350 degrees for 30 minutes or until cooked through. Remove to a serving platter; keep warm. Scrape the pan drippings into a saucepan. Add the sour cream and green chiles. Cook over medium heat until heated through, stirring constantly. Pour over the chicken.

Serves 4

Wine suggestion: Chardonnay, Viognier

Entrées

San Francisco Chicken

Mary Jo McDonald
99.9 KEZ's Mama Jo's
Monday Meal in Minutes

1 package long grain and wild rice mix
1 (10-ounce) can cream of chicken soup
1 (10-ounce) can cream of celery soup
1/4 cup mayonnaise
1 cup milk
1/2 cup slivered almonds
6 boneless skinless chicken breasts

Combine the rice mix, chicken soup, celery soup, mayonnaise and milk in a bowl; mix well. Spoon 2/3 of the mixture into an 8x12-inch baking dish. Arrange the chicken on top. Cover with the remaining soup mixture. Sprinkle almonds over the top. Bake, covered with foil, at 325 degrees for 1 1/2 hours. Remove the foil. Bake for 30 minutes.

Serves 6

Wine suggestion: Chardonnay, Sauvignon Blanc

Spicy Spinach Chicken

1/4 cup crumbled feta cheese
3 tablespoons unsalted butter, softened
1 (10-ounce) package frozen chopped spinach,
thawed, squeezed dry
1 teaspoon minced jalapeño
1 (4- to 5-pound) chicken, cut into 8 pieces
1/4 cup Dijon mustard
1 cup fresh bread crumbs
1 teaspoon salt
1/2 teaspoon pepper
2 tablespoons unsalted butter

Process the first 4 ingredients in a food processor until smooth. Chill for 10 minutes or until firm. Rinse the chicken and pat dry. Cut a pocket between the skin and the meat carefully. Stuff 1 tablespoon of the spinach mixture under the skin. Spread each piece of chicken with Dijon mustard. Place skin side up on a baking sheet. Chill for 30 minutes. Mix the bread crumbs, salt and pepper together. Roll each piece of chicken in the crumbs; return to the baking sheet. Dot with 2 tablespoons butter. Bake at 350 degrees for 1 1/2 hours or until the the chicken is cooked through and the skin is crisp and golden brown.

Serves 4 to 6

Wine suggestion: Châteauneuf-du-Pape Blanc,
Côtes du Rhône Blanc

Entrées

Verde Chile Chicken

1/4 cup butter
2 tablespoon olive oil
14 boneless skinless chicken breasts,
cut into six pieces
Salt and pepper to taste
1 1/2 cups thinly sliced onions
4 cloves of garlic, crushed
2 (7-ounce) cans whole green chiles,
seeded, torn into strips

1 (4-ounce) can chopped green chiles
1 1/2 cups half-and-half
1 teaspoon salt
1/4 teaspoon white pepper
3 cups sour cream
8 cups cooked rice
1 pound Monterey Jack cheese,
thinly sliced

Melt the butter and olive oil in a large skillet over medium-high heat. Season the chicken with salt and pepper. Sauté until golden brown on all sides. Remove to a platter and keep warm. Add the onions and garlic to the skillet. Sauté until the onions are soft. Add the green chile strips. Cook, covered, for 7 to 10 minutes. Combine the chopped green chiles, half-and-half, salt and pepper in a blender container. Process until well mixed. Add the sour cream. Process until smooth. Lightly grease 2 baking dishes. Layer the rice, chicken, onion mixture and sour cream mixture in the prepared baking dishes. Cover with slices of Monterey Jack cheese. Bake at 350 degrees for 45 minutes or until bubbly.

Serves 14

Wine suggestion: Sangría, or serve Mexican beer

Good served with a spinach and mandarin orange salad.
Can be refrigerated for up to 2 days before baking.

Entrées

Medallions of Turkey in

Apple Bourbon Sauce

Robert DeSantis and Edward Hartwig
Samaritan Health Systems

12 ounces toasted bread crumbs
8 ounces walnuts, chopped
8 ounces crumbled bleu cheese
1/4 cup chopped fresh parsley
1/2 cup chopped fresh chives
1/4 teaspoon each white pepper and salt
20 (3-ounce) turkey medallions
3 tablespoons walnut oil
1/2 cup cider vinegar

2 quarts apple juice
1 quart chicken broth
1/2 cup cornstarch
2 tablespoons water
1/4 teaspoon salt
1/4 teaspoon black pepper
5 1/2 ounces bourbon
4 1/2 pounds Granny Smith apples,
chopped

Process the first 7 ingredients in a food processor until coarsely chopped. Sear the turkey in the walnut oil in a large skillet over medium heat until light brown on both sides. Remove to a baking pan. Cover with the bleu cheese mixture. Bake at 350 degrees for 20 minutes or until a meat thermometer registers 160 degrees. Boil the vinegar and apple juice in a saucepan over high heat until reduced to a syrup-like consistency. Heat the chicken broth and a mixture of the cornstarch and water in a large saucepan, mixing well. Boil until thickened. Add to the vinegar mixture; mix well. Add 1/4 teaspoon salt, black pepper and bourbon; mix well. Bring to a boil. Add the apples. Reduce heat and simmer for 2 minutes or until the apples are tender-crisp. Serve the sauce with the turkey.

Serves 10

Wine suggestion: Alsatian Tokay, White Bordeaux, Light Merlot

Entrées

Duck Breasts with

Sage and Jalapeño Polenta

Robert Trick
House of Tricks

6 duck breasts
1 teaspoon each kosher salt and pepper
1 tablespoon olive oil
2 shallots, minced
2 cloves of garlic, minced
2 cups thinly sliced shiitake mushrooms
1 teaspoon grated fresh ginger
1 cup port
6 fresh figs, halved
2 tablespoons butter
Sage and Jalapeño Polenta

Season the duck with salt and pepper, rubbing them into both the skin and flesh side of the meat. Place the duck breasts skin side down in a skillet over medium-high heat. Sauté for 6 to 7 minutes or until brown; turn the breasts over. Sauté for 2 minutes. Remove to a baking pan. Bake at 350 degrees for 10 minutes. Heat the olive oil in a skillet over medium-high heat. Add the shallots and garlic. Cook until the shallots are soft. Add the mushrooms and ginger. Sauté for 2 minutes. Add the port. Cook until the liquid is reduced by 1/3. Add the figs; stir to mix well. Cook until heated through. Remove the skillet from the heat. Stir in the butter. Remove the duck from the oven. Let stand for 5 minutes. Slice the duck. Divide the figs and mushrooms evenly on 6 dinner plates. Arrange the duck over the top. Spoon the sauce over the duck. Serve with Sage and Jalapeño Polenta.

Sage and Jalapeño Polenta

12 cups cold water
1 teaspoon salt
1 teaspoon curry powder
1 chicken bouillon cube (optional)
1 tablespoon butter
2 jalapeños, minced
4 cloves of garlic, minced
3 cups cornmeal
3 cups minced fresh sage leaves
1 cup milk
1 cup grated Parmesan cheese
1 cup mild goat cheese, softened
1 tablespoon olive oil

Combine the water, salt, curry powder, bouillon cube, butter, jalapeños and garlic in a saucepan over high heat. Bring to a boil. Add the cornmeal gradually, whisking constantly. Add the sage; mix well. Reduce the heat to low. Cook for 5 minutes, stirring constantly with a wooden spoon. Add the milk. Stir until well mixed, scraping the polenta from the side of the pan. Cook until the mixture is no longer granular. Add the Parmesan cheese and goat cheese; mix well. Grease a 15x18-inch baking dish with the olive oil. Pour the polenta mixture into the baking dish. Chill for 1 hour or until firm. Invert onto a cutting board. Cut into 15 rounds using a 3-inch biscuit cutter. Place polenta rounds on a nonstick baking sheet. Broil until heated through and light brown.

Serves 6

Wine suggestion: Red Burgundy, Oregon Pinot Noir

Pan-Seared Chilean Sea Bass

With Sun-Dried Blueberry Sauce

Tim Hoobler
Desert Highlands

2 tablespoons julienned zucchini
2 tablespoons julienned red bell pepper
2 tablespoons julienned
green bell pepper
1 tablespoon julienned onion
1/4 cup olive oil
2 cloves of garlic, minced
1 sprig of basil
4 tablespoons tomatoes, peeled,
seeded, chopped

1 (6-ounce) Chilean sea bass
1 tablespoon butter
2 tablespoons chopped shallots
2 tablespoons sun-dried blueberries
1 tablespoon Jerez vinegar
3 tablespoons walnut oil
1 tablespoon chopped fresh basil
2 tablespoons prepared pesto
1 tablespoon reduced balsamic

Sauté the zucchini, red pepper, green pepper and onion individually in the olive oil in a skillet until soft, removing each vegetable when finished. Sauté the garlic in the remaining oil until golden brown. Add the sprig of basil, tomatoes and reserved vegetables. Simmer, covered, for 20 minutes. Sauté the fish in the butter in a skillet over medium-high heat for 5 minutes per side. Add the shallots and blueberries. Cook for 2 minutes. Remove the fish to a plate; keep warm. Deglaze the skillet with the vinegar. Add the walnut oil and chopped basil; mix well. Arrange the fish and vegetables on a plate. Pour the blueberry essence over the fish. Drizzle pesto and balsamic vinegar around the edge of the plate. May increase ingredient amounts for multiple servings.

Serves 1

Wine suggestion: Hermitage Blanc, California Chardonnay, Light Merlot

Entrées

Casco Cod in Potato Crust

Alessandro Stratta
The Phoenician

1 Idaho potato, thinly sliced	¹/₂ cup chopped pancetta
¹/₄ cup clarified butter	1 cup chanterelle mushrooms
4 (5-ounce) cod fillets	2 tablespoons sherry vinegar
Salt and pepper to taste	¹/₂ cup chicken broth
Fork-Mashed Potatoes (page 145)	1 teaspoon dried thyme
¹/₂ cup chopped leeks	1 tablespoon butter
1 teaspoon olive oil	1 tablespoon minced chives

Brush the potato slices with clarified butter. Arrange 6 potato slices on a plate, overlapping the slices. Season the fish fillets with salt and pepper. Place 1 fillet in the center of the potatoes. Wrap the potatoes around the fillet. Repeat the process until all the fillets are wrapped. Chill until ready to use. Heat the remaining clarified butter in a skillet over medium-high heat. Sauté the fish until crisp on both sides. Remove to a baking pan. Bake at 450 degrees for 5 to 7 minutes or until the fish is cooked through. Steam the leeks for 3 minutes. Cook the pancetta in the olive oil in a skillet over medium-high heat for 2 to 3 minutes or until the pancetta begins to brown. Add the steamed leeks and mushrooms; mix well. Add the vinegar. Cook until the mixture is reduced slightly, stirring constantly. Add the broth and thyme. Cook until the mixture is reduced slightly, stirring occasionally. Add the butter; mix well. Remove from the heat. Add the chives; mix well. Place a dollop of Fork-Mashed Potatoes in the center of each of 4 dinner plates. Place 1 fish fillet on top of the potatoes. Spoon the sauce around the potatoes.

Serves 4

Wine suggestion: Sonoma Sauvignon Blanc, Sancerre

Entrées

Tuscan Salmon

2/3 cup dry-packed sun-dried tomatoes
2 cups water
1/8 teaspoon cayenne pepper
2 tablespoons catsup
2 tablespoons tomato paste2
teaspoons capers, drained
2 tablespoons balsamic vinegar
1 1/2 teaspoons minced fresh parsley
1/2 teaspoon tarragon

1 tablespoon minced fresh chives
1/2 teaspoon freshly ground pepper
2 tablespoons lemon juice
1/2 teaspoon minced garlic
2 tablespoons cider vinegar
1/4 cup vegetable oil
4 (8-ounce) salmon steaks

Combine the sun-dried tomatoes and 1 cup of the water in a saucepan over medium-high heat. Simmer for 3 minutes. Drain, reserving the liquid. Chop the tomatoes. Mix with the reserved liquid, next 13 ingredients and 1/2 cup of the water in a bowl. Let stand, covered, for 2 to 12 hours. Place the salmon in a large shallow baking dish. Transfer 1/2 of the tomato mixture to a small bowl. Add the remaining 1/2 cup water; mix well. Pour over the salmon; turn to coat. Marinate in the refrigerator for 2 hours. Grill the salmon over hot coals for 13 to 15 minutes or until cooked through, basting often with the marinade. Serve with the remaining tomato mixture.

Serves 4

Wine suggestion: Chardonnay, Light Merlot

Pan-Seared Salmon with

Mango Vinaigrette

Richard Sederholt
Remington's Restaurant at The Scottsdale Plaza Resort

¹/₂ cup dry bread crumbs
1 tablespoon grated fresh horseradish,
or prepared horseradish
1 tablespoon chopped fresh herbs,
such as basil and cilantro
1 tablespoon olive oil
¹/₈ teaspoon salt

Salt and freshly ground pepper to taste
1 cup peeled chopped fresh mango
1 tablespoon sake (optional)
3 tablespoons rice wine vinegar
4 (7-ounce) salmon fillets,
pin bones removed
2 tablespoons olive oil

Combine the bread crumbs, horseradish, herbs, 1 tablespoon olive oil, ¹/₈ teaspoon salt and pepper to taste in a blender container. Process until smooth; set aside. Combine the mango, sake, wine vinegar and salt and pepper to taste in a blender container. Process until smooth. Season the salmon with salt and pepper. Heat 2 tablespoons olive oil in a large skillet over medium-high heat. Sear the salmon for 2 minutes per side or until brown. Transfer the salmon to a greased ovenproof pan. Bake at 350 degrees for 10 minutes or just until cooked through. Remove from the oven. Coat the salmon with horseradish crumbs. Return to the oven. Cook for 2 to 3 minutes. Ladle mango vinaigrette in the center of each of 4 dinner plates. Center 1 salmon fillet in the vinaigrette on each plate. Serve immediately.

Serves 4

Wine Suggestion: California Chardonnay or a light Merlot

Skillet-Seared Swordfish with

Smoked Ham and Bean Salad

Robert McGrath
The Roaring Fork

2 cups blanched haricot vert (thin green beans)
1 cup blanched wax beans
1/2 cup cooked white beans
1 cup julienned smoked ham hock
1 cup julienned red onions
1 tablespoon olive oil
Kosher salt and cracked pepper to taste
1/2 cup freshly squeezed lemon juice

2 tablespoons extra-virgin olive oil
1 tablespoon chopped fresh thyme
1 teaspoon chopped garlic
4 (8-ounce) center-cut swordfish steaks
2 tablespoons olive oil
8 sweet potato chips (Terra Chips)
2 tablespoons grated lemon peel
4 sprigs of thyme
2 tablespoons chipotle chile oil

Sauté the haricot vert, wax beans, white beans, ham and onions in 1 tablespoon olive oil in a skillet over medium-high heat until the onions are soft. Season with Kosher salt and pepper; set aside. Whisk the lemon juice, 2 tablespoons olive oil, thyme and garlic in a bowl until well mixed; set aside. Season the fish with salt and pepper. Use a paper towel to wipe a cast-iron skillet with olive oil. Sear the fish in the skillet over medium-high heat for 1 1/2 to 2 minutes on each side. Place a mound of bean salad on each of 4 dinner plates. Place 2 sweet potato chips in each mound of salad. Place the fish against the salad. Spoon the lemon vinaigrette over the fish and salad. Place a thyme sprig on the potatoes. Sprinkle lemon peel over the fish. Drizzle the chipotle oil around the perimeter of each plate.

Serves 4

Wine suggestion: Rhinegau, Kabinett Riesling, California Chardonnay

Entrées

Grilled Tuna with

Spinach and Tomatoes

¹/₂ cup butter
4 cups fresh spinach leaves
1 cup blanched haricot vert (thin green beans)
¹/₂ cup canned black beans, rinsed
¹/₂ cup chopped tomatoes
¹/₄ cup chopped fresh cilantro
2 tablespoons lemon juice
1 tablespoon capers, rinsed
Salt and pepper to taste
4 (6-ounce) tuna steaks
Olive oil to taste
1 tablespoon chopped fresh thyme

Melt the butter in a large skillet over medium-high heat. Cook until the butter begins to brown. Remove the skillet from the heat. Add the spinach, haricot vert, black beans, tomatoes, cilantro, lemon juice and capers; toss to mix well. Season with salt and pepper; keep warm. Brush the tuna steaks with olive oil. Sprinkle thyme, salt and pepper over both sides of the fish. Broil or grill for 3 minutes per side or until opaque. Cut into ¹/₂-inch slices. Place a mound of spinach mixture on each of 4 plates. Top with sliced tuna. Serve immediately.

Serves 4

Wine suggestion: Light Pinot Noir, Light Merlot, Light Chateauneuf-du-Pape

Entrées

Princess Paella

Reed Groban
Scottsdale Princess

2 tablespoons Spanish olive oil
2 teaspoons chopped garlic
1/2 cup chopped onion
6 chistora (Spanish summer sausage),
cut into 1/2-inch pieces
6 escargot
4 boneless skinless chicken breasts, cut
into 1 1/2-inch pieces
3 ounces pork, cut into 1 1/2-inch pieces
3/4 cup chopped tomatoes
2 cups rice
4 1/2 cups chicken broth

8 to 10 saffron threads
2 jumbo shrimp
4 black mussels
4 cocktail clams
1 (1 1/4-pound) lobster, split (optional)
3 tablespoons chopped
red bell peppers
3 tablespoons chopped
green bell peppers
1/4 cup white wine
3 tablespoons fresh green peas

Heat the olive oil in a large skillet over medium-high heat. Add the garlic, onions, chistora, escargot, chicken and pork. Sauté until the onion is soft. Add the tomatoes, rice, broth and saffron. Cook until the rice begins to soften. Add the shrimp, mussels and clams. Cook for 2 to 3 minutes. Add the lobster, red peppers, green peppers and wine. Cook until the liquid is absorbed. Remove from the heat; cover. Let rest for 3 to 5 minutes. Sprinkle green peas over the top.

Serves 2

Wine suggestion: California Cabernet Franc, Hermitage Blanc

Entrées

Pan-Roasted Mussels with

Red Curry and Smoked Bacon

Robert McGrath
The Roaring Fork

48 "Mediterranean Blue" mussels from Washington State, or black mussels
2 tablespoons butter
6 ounces hickory-smoked bacon, chopped
1 cup chopped leeks, white part only
$^1/_2$ cup chopped fennel bulb
$1^1/_2$ cups sliced button mushrooms

2 cups drained chopped plum tomatoes
2 tablespoons chopped garlic
1 tablespoon plus 1 teaspoon red curry paste
Salt and pepper to taste
$^3/_4$ cup dry white wine
1 cup chopped fresh mint

Scrub the mussels. Pull off the beards just before cooking. Melt the butter in a heavy nonreactive pan over medium heat. Add the bacon and cook until medium crisp. Add the leeks, fennel and mushrooms. Cook until the leeks and fennel are soft. Add the tomatoes, garlic and curry paste. Season with salt and pepper. Add the white wine; mix well. Add the mussels. Cook, covered, over high heat until all of the mussels have opened, shaking the pan occasionally. Sprinkle fresh mint over the mussels; stir. Serve in shallow bowls with broth and vegetables.

Serves 4

Wine suggestion: Bordeaux Blanc, Alsatian Riesling

Entrées

Pasta with Scallops and

Lemony Mustard Sauce

1 cup white wine
¹/₂ teaspoon grated lemon peel
¹/₂ pound bay scallops
2 teaspoons Dijon mustard
5 tablespoons butter
Salt and pepper to taste
5 ounces angel hair pasta
1 tablespoon chopped fresh chives

Combine the wine and lemon peel in a skillet over medium heat. Simmer until heated through. Add the scallops. Cook until almost opaque. Remove the scallops with a slotted spoon to a bowl; set aside. Boil the remaining liquid in the skillet until reduced to ¹/₄ cup. Reduce the heat to low. Add the mustard; whisk to mix well. Add 4 tablespoons of the butter 1 piece at a time, whisking constantly. Add the reserved scallops with their juices, salt and pepper; stir. Cook until heated through. Cook the pasta in boiling salted water until al dente; drain. Toss with the remaining 1 tablespoon of butter. Divide the pasta between 2 plates. Spoon scallop mixture over the top. Sprinkle with chives.

Serves 2

Wine suggestion: Vouvray or Dry Chenin Blanc

Entrées

Portuguese Shrimp and Scallops

3 tablespoons butter
3 tablespoons olive oil
6 cloves of garlic, minced
1 pound sliced mushrooms
2 tablespoons tomato paste
$^1/_4$ cup white wine
$^1/_4$ cup freshly squeezed lemon juice
1 pound medium-size shrimp, peeled, deveined
1 bunch green onions, chopped
1 pound bay scallops
Salt and pepper to taste
$^1/_4$ cup chopped parsley

Melt the butter and oil in a large skillet over medium heat. Add the garlic. Sauté for 1 minute. Increase the heat to high. Add the mushrooms. Sauté until the mushrooms are soft. Add the tomato paste; stir to mix well. Add the wine and lemon juice. Bring to a boil. Add the shrimp and green onions. Cook for 1 minute, stirring continuously. Add the scallops. Cook for 3 minutes or until the shrimp and scallops are opaque, stirring continuously. Season with salt and pepper. Sprinkle parsley over the mixture. May be served over rice.

Serves 6

Wine suggestion: Chardonnay

Malay Shrimp Satay

1/4 cup vegetable oil
1/4 cup sliced green onions
4 cloves of garlic, minced
1 1/2 cups chicken broth
6 tablespoons peanut butter
2 tablespoons soy sauce
1 teaspoon grated lemon peel
1/2 teaspoon cayenne pepper
2 tablespoons freshly squeezed lemon juice
2 teaspoons chili powder
1 teaspoon packed light brown sugar
1/2 teaspoon ground ginger
1 pound shrimp, shelled, deveined, tails intact

Heat the oil in a large skillet over medium-high heat. Add the onions and garlic. Sauté until the onions are soft. Add the broth, peanut butter, soy sauce, lemon peel, cayenne, lemon juice, chili powder, brown sugar and ginger; mix well. Simmer for 10 minutes, stirring often. Remove from the heat; cool. Skim and discard any fat that rises to the surface. Transfer half the mixture to a bowl. Add the shrimp, turning to coat. Let stand for 1 hour, turning once or twice. Discard the marinade, reserving the shrimp. Broil or grill the shrimp until opaque. Heat the reserved peanut mixture. Serve shrimp with remaining peanut mixture on the side.

Serves 8

Wine suggestion: Alsatian Tokay, Gewurztraminer

Skewer the shrimp for easier grilling.
This dish is also marvelous as an appetizer.

Entrées

Shrimp Enchiladas with

Goat Cheese and Chipotle Cream

Vincent Guerithault
Vincent's on Camelback

1 medium leek, sliced, blanched
and drained
4 ounces goat cheese
$1/2$ cup heavy cream
Salt and pepper
1 teaspoon olive oil

12 medium-size shrimp, peeled,
deveined
4 (8-inch) flour tortillas
1 cup heavy cream
1 tablespoon chipotle in adobo sauce
(available in specialty stores)

Cook the leek, goat cheese, cream, salt and pepper in a saucepan over medium heat for 5 minutes. Cook for 2 minutes over low heat. Sauté the shrimp in olive oil in a skillet over medium-high heat for 1 minute. Spoon 2 shrimp and $1/4$ of the cream sauce in the middle of each tortilla. Fold the tortilla to enclose the filling. Secure with a wooden pick. Combine the cream and chipotle in adobo sauce in a small saucepan over medium heat. Cook until slightly thickened, stirring frequently. Simmer the tortillas in chipotle cream for 5 minutes. Remove the picks. Serve hot with chipotle cream around the tortilla and the remaining shrimp arranged on top.

Serves 4

Wine suggestion: Cotes du Rhone Blanc or fresh blended margaritas

Entrées

Pasta with Asparagus and

Pine Nuts

2 tablespoons butter
2 cups chopped mushrooms
1/4 cup chopped onion
1 clove of garlic, crushed
1 pound asparagus, steamed
3/4 cup heavy cream
12 ounces pasta, cooked
4 teaspoons toasted pine nuts
Shredded Parmesan cheese to taste

Melt the butter in a saucepan over medium-high heat. Add the mushrooms and onion. Sauté until the onion is soft and the liquid from the mushrooms has been absorbed. Add the garlic. Sauté for 1 minute. Add the asparagus and cream; stir to mix well. Bring to a boil. Pour over pasta. Sprinkle pine nuts and Parmesan cheese over the top.

Serves 4

Wine suggestion: Sauvignon Blanc

This is easy, and everyone likes it—even the kids.

Entrées

Angel Hair Pasta with

Grilled Portobello Mushrooms

Michael de Maria
Michael's

2 tablespoons olive oil
2 tablespoons sliced garlic
3/4 teaspoon chopped shallots
4 Grilled Portobello Mushrooms,
sliced into strips (page 148)
2 red bell peppers, roasted, peeled,
seeded, julienned
1/2 cup chicken broth

1/2 cup Mushroom Stock (page 147)
Salt and pepper to taste
1 1/2 pounds angel hair pasta,
cooked al dente
2 tablespoons butter
2 cups fresh spinach,
cut into strips
2 tablespoons chopped parsley

Heat the olive oil in a large skillet over medium-high heat. Add the garlic and shallots. Sauté until the shallots are soft. Add the Grilled Portobello Mushrooms and red peppers. Sauté for 1 minute. Add the chicken broth. Cook for 5 minutes. Add the Mushroom Stock, salt and pepper. Cook for 2 minutes. Add the hot pasta, butter and spinach; toss well. Top with the parsley.

Serves 4

Wine suggestion: Barbera, Chianti Classico, California Sangiovese

An elegant vegetarian entrée.

Entrées

Cannelloni Casserole

8 ounces lasagna noodles,
cooked, drained
1 pound spinach, chopped
2 tablespoons melted butter or
margarine
1 cup small curd cottage cheese
1/4 teaspoon nutmeg
1/4 teaspoon basil
2 tablespoons grated Parmesan cheese
2 eggs, beaten
1/2 teaspoon salt

1/8 teaspoon pepper
1/4 cup butter or margarine
1/4 cup flour
1/2 teaspoon salt
1/4 teaspoon cayenne pepper
2 cups milk
1/2 cup grated Parmesan cheese
3 tablespoons crushed garlic croutons
3 tablespoons grated Parmesan cheese
Butter or margarine to taste

Cut each lasagna noodle in half crosswise. Rinse the spinach. Place the undrained spinach in a saucepan over low heat. Cook, covered, for 5 minutes; drain and cool. Combine the spinach, 2 tablespoons butter, cottage cheese, nutmeg, basil, Parmesan cheese, eggs, salt and pepper in a bowl; mix well. Place 1 tablespoon of the spinach mixture in the center of each reserved lasagna noodle. Roll the lasagna to enclose the filling. Place seam side down in a 12x7 1/2-inch baking pan. Combine 1/4 cup butter, flour, salt and cayenne in a saucepan over low heat. Cook until the mixture is smooth and bubbly, stirring constantly. Add the milk gradually, stirring constantly. Add 1/2 cup Parmesan cheese. Boil for 1 minute, stirring constantly. Pour sauce over cannelloni rolls. Combine the crushed croutons and Parmesan cheese. Sprinkle over the top of the cannelloni rolls. Dot with butter to taste. Bake at 425 degrees for 15 minutes or until light brown and bubbly.

Serves 4 to 6

Wine suggestion: Pinot Grigio

Entrées

Carbonara

1 pound bacon, chopped
8 cloves of garlic, minced
2 (6-ounce) cans mushroom pieces, drained
6 ounces Canadian bacon, chopped
1 cup dry white wine
1 pound capellini, broken into thirds
4 eggs, beaten
$^1/_2$ cup heavy cream
1 $^1/_2$ cups grated Parmesan cheese
$^1/_4$ teaspoon pepper

Combine the bacon and 5 of the minced cloves of garlic in a large saucepan over medium heat. Cook until the bacon is brown. Add the mushrooms; mix well. Cook until the mushrooms begin to brown, stirring occasionally. Add the Canadian bacon; mix well. Add the remaining garlic and wine when the Canadian bacon begins to brown. Reduce the heat. Cook, covered, for 15 to 20 minutes. Cook the cappellini according to package directions. Combine the eggs and cream in a large bowl; whisk to mix well. Add $^1/_2$ of the Parmesan cheese; whisk to mix well. Drain the capellini. Add to the egg mixture; toss to mix well. Add the pepper; mix well. Add the hot bacon mixture and remaining Parmesan cheese; toss to mix well. Serve immediately.

Serves 8

Wine suggestion: Chianti Classico Reserva or Orvietto

You'll never have leftovers!

Side Dishes

Prosciutto Almond Asparagus

2 ounces thinly sliced prosciutto, cut into $^1/_3$-inch pieces
1 tablespoon olive oil
$^1/_3$ cup sliced almonds
$^3/_4$ cup freshly squeezed orange juice
$^1/_3$ cup red wine vinegar
1 teaspoon cornstarch
1 teaspoon grated orange peel
2 pounds asparagus, ends trimmed
$^1/_2$ cup water
Pepper to taste

Combine the prosciutto and olive oil in a large skillet over medium heat. Sauté for 4 minutes or until the prosciutto is brown. Remove the prosciutto to paper towels with a slotted spoon; drain. Add the almonds to the drippings. Sauté 2 to 3 minutes or until golden brown. Remove the almonds to paper towels with a slotted spoon; drain. Discard the drippings. Wipe the skillet clean with paper towels. Combine the orange juice, vinegar, cornstarch and orange peel in a bowl. Stir until the cornstarch is dissolved. Pour into the skillet. Cook over high heat for 1 minute or until bubbly. Transfer to a small bowl; keep warm. Rinse the skillet. Place the asparagus in the skillet with the water. Simmer, covered, for 2 to 4 minutes or until the asparagus is tender-crisp, stirring once. Arrange the asparagus on a serving platter. Pour the orange sauce over the asparagus. Scatter prosciutto and almonds on top. Season with pepper. Garnish with an orange twist.

Serves 6

Cheesy Lemon Artichokes

2 (14-ounce) cans artichoke bottoms,
drained, rinsed
1½ cups grated Parmesan cheese
½ cup mayonnaise
1½ tablespoons freshly squeezed lemon juice
4 cloves of garlic, minced
1 teaspoon grated lemon peel
Salt and pepper to taste
⅓ cup pine nuts

Grease an 8-inch baking pan. Arrange the artichokes on the bottom of the pan, rounded side down. Combine the Parmesan cheese, mayonnaise, lemon juice, garlic, lemon peel, salt and pepper in a bowl; mix well. Place a mound of the Parmesan cheese mixture in each artichoke. Sprinkle pine nuts over the Parmesan cheese mixture. Bake at 375 degrees for 20 minutes or until heated through. Garnish with chopped parsley.

Serves 16

Granny Annie's Gourmet Beans

12 slices bacon, chopped
1 green bell pepper, chopped
1 bunch green onions, chopped
¾ cup packed light brown sugar
½ (12-ounce) bottle chili sauce
1 (16-ounce) can pork and beans, drained
1 (16-ounce) can pinto beans, drained
1 (16-ounce) can French-style
green beans, drained
1 (16-ounce) can red kidney beans, drained

Combine the bacon, green pepper and green onions in a saucepan over medium heat. Cook until the onions are soft. Add the brown sugar and chili sauce; mix well. Add the pork and beans, pinto beans, green beans and kidney beans; mix well. Cook, covered, over low heat for 1 hour.

Serves 12

This is a great accompaniment for ham.

Hot Green Beans Caesar

3 tablespoons vegetable oil
³/₄ cup ¹/₂-inch bread cubes
I tablespoon vinegar
I teaspoon minced onion
¹/₄ teaspoon salt
I (16-ounce) can cut green beans, drained
2 to 3 tablespoons grated Parmesan cheese

Heat 2 tablespoons of the oil in a skillet over medium-high heat. Add the bread cubes. Sauté until golden and crisp. Combine the vinegar, remaining oil, onion and salt in a bowl; mix well. Add the green beans to the bread cubes, stirring once. Pour the oil mixture over the green bean mixture. Cook, stirring, until heated through. Sprinkle with Parmesan cheese. Serve immediately.

Serves 4

A side-dish twist on the famous salad, these beans are an ideal accompaniment to seafood.

Broccoli Bacon Bake

6 tablespoons butter
6 tablespoons flour
2 cups milk
¹/₄ teaspoon salt
I cup shredded sharp cheese
6 slices bacon, cooked, crumbled
I cup sliced mushrooms
¹/₂ cup slivered almonds
2 (10-ounce) packages frozen chopped broccoli, thawed, drained

Melt the butter in a saucepan over medium heat. Add the flour. Cook, stirring constantly, until bubbly. Add the milk slowly, stirring constantly. Cook until thickened, stirring constantly. Add the salt and cheese; mix well. Add the bacon, mushrooms and almonds; mix well. Add the broccoli; mix well. Pour the mixture into a greased 1¹/₂-quart casserole. Bake at 350 degrees for I hour.

Serves 6 to 8

Side Dishes

Calypso Cabbage

8 cups shredded red cabbage
2 McIntosh apples, chopped
I cup white grape juice, or I cup water
plus 4 tablespoons sugar
I teaspoon salt, or to taste
4 whole cloves
I tablespoon balsamic vinegar
¹/₄ cup butter
2 tablespoons currant jelly
¹/₈ teaspoon cayenne

Combine the cabbage, apples, grape juice, salt and cloves in a large nonreactive saucepan over medium heat. Simmer, covered, for 45 minutes or until the cabbage is tender and the apples are very soft. Remove and discard the cloves. Add the vinegar, butter, jelly and cayenne; mix well. Cook until heated through. Adjust seasonings.

Serves 6

Company Carrots

2 bunches baby carrots
¹/₂ cup (or a little more) mayonnaise
I tablespoon minced onion
I tablespoon prepared horseradish
Salt and pepper to taste
2 tablespoons butter
¹/₂ cup fine cracker crumbs

Cook the carrots in water to cover in a saucepan over medium heat until tender-crisp; drain, reserving ¹/₂ cup cooking water. Arrange the carrots in a buttered baking dish. Combine the reserved cooking water, mayonnaise, onion, horseradish, salt and pepper in a bowl; mix well. Pour over the carrots. Dot with butter. Sprinkle cracker crumbs over the top. Bake at 375 degrees for 15 to 20 minutes or until bubbly.

Serves 6

*Makes a delicious accompaniment to roasted meats
and can be prepared ahead.*

Mexican Corn Casserole

8 ounces cream cheese, softened
1/4 cup margarine or butter, softened
3 tablespoons flour
1/4 cup milk
3 (12-ounce) cans white corn, drained
1 (7-ounce) can chopped green chiles
Salt and pepper to taste

Melt the cream cheese and margarine in a saucepan over medium heat; mix well. Add the flour and milk; stir to mix well. Cook until thickened, stirring constantly. Remove the saucepan from the heat. Add the corn, green chiles, salt and pepper; mix well. Pour into an ovenproof casserole. Bake, covered, at 375 degrees for 30 to 40 minutes or until bubbly.

Serves 8

Mexican Spoon Bread

1 (16-ounce) can cream-style corn
3/4 cup milk
1/3 cup vegetable oil
2 eggs
1 cup yellow cornmeal
1/2 teaspoon baking soda
1 teaspoon salt
1 (4-ounce) can chopped green chiles
2 cups shredded longhorn cheese or
Cheddar cheese

Combine the corn, milk, oil, eggs, cornmeal, baking soda and salt in a mixer bowl. Beat until well mixed. Pour 1/2 of the mixture into a buttered 1 1/2-quart casserole. Sprinkle green chiles and 1 cup of the cheese over the corn mixture. Spoon the remaining corn mixture over the cheese. Top with remaining cheese. Bake at 400 degrees for 45 minutes or until puffed and golden.

Serves 4

A Southwestern classic.

Spaghetti Squash Supreme

2 to 3 pounds spaghetti squash
2 cups shredded fresh spinach leaves
3 tablespoons lemon juice
5 tablespoons butter
1 clove of garlic, minced
2 tablespoons minced shallots
1 cup thinly sliced mushrooms
2 tablespoons brandy
1 cup heavy cream
Salt and pepper to taste
6 slices bacon, cooked, crumbled
1/4 cup grated Parmesan cheese
8 whole spinach leaves

Cut the squash into halves lengthwise; remove and discard the seeds. Place the squash in a large pot with 3 inches of water. Boil, covered, for 25 minutes or until tender. Remove the squash to a plate to cool. Scoop the insides of the squash into a bowl using a fork. Cook the shredded spinach in boiling salted water for 3 minutes or until tender; drain well. Add the lemon juice; toss to mix and set aside. Melt the butter in a large skillet over medium heat. Add the garlic and shallots. Cook for 3 minutes. Add the mushrooms. Cook for 5 minutes. Add the brandy and cream. Bring to a boil. Remove the skillet from the heat. Add the spaghetti squash and cooked spinach. Season with salt and pepper. Add the bacon and Parmesan cheese; toss to mix well. Place 2 spinach leaves on each of 4 plates. Top with the spaghetti squash mixture. Serve immediately. Serve with grilled lamb or veal chops.

Serves 4

Marvelous, even for those who avoid squash.

Oven-Roasted Red Onions

6 large red onions, skin on
Olive oil
Salt and pepper to taste
1/3 cup red wine vinegar

Coat each onion with olive oil. Place in a roasting pan suitable for stove-top cooking. Sprinkle each onion with salt and pepper. Bake at 375 degrees for 1 1/2 to 2 hours or until the onions are soft. Remove the onions to a bowl; set aside. Place the roasting pan over medium-high heat. Add the wine vinegar to the pan drippings. Cook for 2 minutes, scraping the brown bits from the bottom of the roasting pan. Cut the onions in half horizontally. Brush the wine vinegar mixture over the cut sides.

Serves 6

Vidalia Onion Pie

2 tablespoons butter
2 cups thinly sliced Vidalia onions
1 unbaked (9-inch) pie shell
3/4 cup milk
2 eggs
1 teaspoon salt
Pepper to taste
3/4 cup Gruyère cheese or Swiss cheese
1/8 teaspoon paprika

Melt the butter in a skillet over medium heat. Sauté the onions for 12 minutes or until soft. Arrange the onions in the pie shell. Combine the milk, eggs, salt and pepper in a bowl; beat until well mixed. Pour egg mixture over the onions. Sprinkle the Gruyère cheese over the egg mixture. Sprinkle paprika over the top. Bake at 350 degrees for 35 minutes or until a knife inserted in the center comes out clean. Garnish with chopped parsley.

Serves 6

Four Cheese Potatoes

12 medium red potatoes, cut into 1-inch cubes
8 ounces shredded mozzarella cheese
$^1/_3$ cup grated Parmesan cheese
2 cups ricotta cheese
1 cup sour cream
3 cups shredded Cheddar cheese
$^1/_4$ cup chopped green onions
3 tablespoons chopped parsley
1 teaspoon basil
$^1/_4$ teaspoon pepper
2 cloves of garlic, minced

Cook the potatoes in boiling water in a saucepan over medium-high heat for 10 minutes or until tender-crisp; drain. Combine the mozzarella cheese, Parmesan cheese, ricotta cheese, sour cream, 1$^1/_2$ cups of the Cheddar cheese, onions, parsley, basil, pepper and garlic in a large mixer bowl; toss to mix well. Add the potatoes; mix well. Transfer the mixture to a greased 9x13-inch casserole. Sprinkle the remaining Cheddar cheese over the top. Bake at 350 degrees for 30 minutes or until bubbly.

Serves 8 to 10

Side Dishes

Potatoes au Beurre

6 to 8 medium baking potatoes, peeled
2 to 3 teaspoons salt
$1/8$ teaspoon pepper
5 tablespoons minced parsley
1 cup shredded sharp Cheddar cheese
6 tablespoons butter
1 cup heavy cream

Cut the potatoes into $1/2$-inch strips, resembling French fries. Layer the potatoes in a 9x13-inch baking dish. Sprinkle with salt, pepper, 3 tablespoons of the parsley and cheese. Dot with butter. Pour the cream over all. Sprinkle with the remaining 2 tablespoons parsley. Bake, covered, at 350 degrees for $1^1/_2$ hours. Remove the cover. Bake for 30 minutes or until brown.

Serves 6 to 8

Roasted New Potatoes

$1/4$ cup melted butter
$1/2$ teaspoon marjoram leaves
$1/2$ teaspoon salt
$1/4$ teaspoon pepper
2 pounds red new potatoes
3 small onions, cut into quarters

Pour the butter into a 2-quart casserole. Add the marjoram, salt and pepper; mix well. Add the potatoes; turn to coat. Add the onions; mix well. Bake, covered, at 400 degrees for 45 minutes to 1 hour or until the potatoes are tender, stirring once.

Serves 8 to 10

Potluck Potato Casserole

1 (2-pound) package frozen hash brown
potatoes, partially thawed
1 (10-ounce) can cream of chicken soup
³/4 cup melted butter
1 teaspoon salt
¹/4 teaspoon pepper
¹/2 cup chopped onion
2 cups sour cream
2 cups shredded Cheddar cheese
2 cups crushed cornflakes

Combine the potatoes, soup, ¹/2 cup of the butter, salt, pepper, onion, sour cream and cheese in a bowl; mix well. Pour into a buttered 9x13-inch baking dish. Combine the cornflakes and remaining butter in a small bowl; mix well. Sprinkle over the potatoes. Bake at 350 degrees for 45 minutes.

Serves 12 to 15

Marvelous at brunch. Popular time after time.

Fork-Mashed Potatoes

Alessandro Stratta
The Phoenician

8 Yukon gold potatoes
¹/2 gallon water
1 bulb of garlic, split
2 tablespoons thyme
1 tablespoon black peppercorns
2 bay leaves
¹/4 cup chopped onion
1¹/2 teaspoons coarse salt
¹/4 cup extra-virgin olive oil
¹/4 cup butter
¹/4 cup Italian parsley leaves
Salt and pepper to taste

Combine the potatoes, water, garlic, thyme, peppercorns, bay leaves, onion and salt in a large saucepan over high heat. Bring to a boil. Reduce the heat. Simmer for 30 to 35 minutes or until the potatoes are tender. Remove the potatoes with a slotted spoon; cool slightly. Peel the potatoes. Combine the potatoes, olive oil and butter in a bowl. Mash the potatoes with a fork. Add the parsley, salt and pepper; mix well.

Serves 4

Serve with Casco Cod in Potato Crust (page 119).

Huggo's Asian Mushrooms

1 to 2 tablespoons butter
6 ounces fresh, wild shiitake, oyster or crimini
mushrooms, julienned
1 tablespoon sliced green onions
1 tablespoon chopped lemon grass
1/8 teaspoon Indonesian chili paste (optional)
1/8 teaspoon minced garlic
1/8 teaspoon minced fresh ginger
1 tablespoon soy sauce
1/4 cup dry sherry

Melt the butter in a wok or skillet over medium-high heat. Add the mushrooms, green onions, lemon grass, chili paste, garlic, ginger and soy sauce. Stir-fry until the mushrooms are tender. Add the sherry; stir to mix well. Serve immediately.

Serves 2

Mushroom-Stuffed Tomatoes

6 medium tomatoes
3 tablespoons butter or margarine
1 1/2 cups chopped fresh mushrooms
1/2 cup sour cream
2 egg yolks, beaten
1/4 cup plus 3 tablespoons fine bread crumbs
1 teaspoon salt
1/8 teaspoon pepper
1/8 teaspoon thyme

Cut and discard the stem end from the tomatoes. Scoop out and reserve the pulp. Turn the shells upside down to drain. Chop the pulp finely, reserving 1 cup; set aside. Melt 2 tablespoons of the butter in a skillet over medium heat. Sauté the mushrooms until tender. Combine the sour cream and egg yolks in a small bowl; whisk to mix well. Add sour cream mixture and reserved tomato pulp to the mushrooms; mix well. Add 1/4 cup of the crumbs, salt, pepper and thyme. Cook until the mixture boils and thickens, stirring constantly. Arrange the tomato shells in a 10x6x1 1/2-inch baking dish. Spoon mushroom mixture into the tomato shells. Combine the remaining butter and bread crumbs in a small bowl; mix well. Sprinkle on top of each tomato shell. Bake at 375 degrees for 25 minutes.

Serves 6

Mushroom Barley Casserole

1/3 cup butter
2/3 cup chopped onion
2/3 cup sliced celery
1 cup pearled barley
1 (10-ounce) can cream of mushroom soup
2 cups water
1/4 cup chopped parsley, or
2 tablespoons dried

Grease an 8x8-inch baking dish. Melt the butter in a skillet over medium-high heat. Add the onion and celery. Sauté until the onion is soft. Add the barley. Cook for 2 minutes or until the barley is light golden brown, stirring frequently. Combine the soup, water and parsley in a bowl; mix well. Add the barley mixture; mix well. Pour into the prepared baking dish. Bake, covered, at 350 degrees for 1 1/4 hours or until the liquid is absorbed. Stir before serving.

Serves 6 to 8

One half pound of sliced fresh mushrooms may be sautéed with the onion and celery.

Mushroom Stock

Michael de Maria
Michael's

1 1/2 teaspoons olive oil
3/4 pound mushrooms, chopped
1/4 cup chopped onion
1/2 carrot, sliced
1/2 clove of garlic, minced
1/4 teaspoon black peppercorns
2 tablespoons chopped fresh parsley
1 tablespoon chopped fresh sage
6 cups chicken broth
1/2 cup butter, cut into pieces
1/8 teaspoon salt

Heat the olive oil in a saucepan over medium-high heat. Add the mushrooms, onion, carrot and garlic. Sauté for 10 minutes or until the vegetables begin to caramelize. Add the peppercorns, parsley, sage and broth. Bring to a boil. Reduce the heat. Simmer for 40 minutes or until the mixture is reduced by half. Whisk the butter into the stock one piece at a time. Season with salt.

Serves 4

See recipe using Mushroom Stock on page 131.

Grilled Portobello Mushrooms

Michael de Maria
Michael's

2 tablespoons balsamic vinegar
$1/4$ cup olive oil
1 teaspoon chopped garlic
1 teaspoon chopped fresh rosemary
1 teaspoon salt
1 teaspoon pepper
4 large portobello mushrooms

Combine the vinegar, olive oil, garlic, rosemary, salt and pepper in a bowl; mix well. Remove and discard the stems from the mushrooms. Add the mushroom caps to the oil mixture; turn to coat. Marinate for 1 hour. Remove the mushrooms from the marinade. Broil or grill until tender. Remove to a container with a tightfitting lid. Let stand, covered, until cool.

Serves 4

See recipe using Grilled Portobello Mushrooms on page 131.

Spicy Thai Noodles

3 to 4 tablespoons peanut butter
1 to 2 tablespoons sesame sauce (tahini)
1 teaspoon salt
4 teaspoons sugar
$1/4$ cup light soy sauce
2 tablespoons wine vinegar
$1/4$ cup sesame oil
2 teaspoons cayenne
4 cloves of garlic, minced
$1/4$ cup chopped green onions
1 pound spaghetti, cooked, drained

Combine the peanut butter, sesame sauce, salt, sugar, soy sauce, wine vinegar, sesame oil, cayenne, garlic and green onions in a bowl; mix well. Pour over spaghetti; toss to coat. Garnish with chopped cucumber, water chestnuts, chopped carrots, bamboo shoots, bean sprouts or chopped green onions.

Serves 6 to 8

Serve hot or cold, as an entrée or a side dish. Add sliced chicken. It's great.

Side Dishes

Penne Margherita

6 tablespoons extra-virgin olive oil
4 cloves of garlic, chopped
4 medium tomatoes, peeled, chopped
1 small bunch fresh basil, chopped
1 cup shredded mozzarella
$1/8$ teaspoon oregano
1 pound penne, cooked, drained
1 cup grated Parmesan cheese

Combine the olive oil, garlic, tomatoes, basil, mozzarella cheese and oregano in a large bowl; toss to mix well. Add the hot pasta; toss to mix well. Add the Parmesan cheese; toss to mix well. Serve immediately.

Serves 4

Tasty as a side dish or vegetarian entrée, this pasta is very easy and very good.

Kaleidoscope Rice Casserole

2 cups brown rice
$4^{1}/_{4}$ cups water
1 envelope onion soup mix
Thinly sliced carrots to taste
Thinly sliced celery to taste
Halved cherry tomatoes to taste
Sliced avocado to taste
Sliced Muenster cheese to taste

Combine the brown rice, water and onion soup mix in a saucepan over medium heat. Cook according to the directions on the rice package. Spread the cooked rice in a shallow casserole. Top with carrots, celery, tomatoes, avocado and cheese. Broil until the cheese is melted.

Serves 4 to 6

This casserole is very colorful and serves as a lovely side dish for a dinner party. You can substitute wild rice for part of the brown rice, if desired.

Green Chile Pilaf

Barbara Pool Fenzl
Les Gourmettes Cooking School

1 pound tomatillos, husked, washed, quartered
2 large jalapeño peppers, seeded, chopped
2 cups water
$1/2$ cup chopped onion
2 cups chopped cilantro stems and leaves
1 tablespoon salt
6 poblano chiles, roasted, peeled, seeded
5 romaine lettuce leaves
4 green onions, chopped
6 cloves of garlic, peeled
$1/4$ cup olive oil
3 cups long grain rice, rinsed

Combine the tomatillos, jalapeño peppers and water in a blender container. Process until chunky. Add the onion, cilantro, salt, chiles, lettuce, green onions and garlic. Process for 2 minutes or until smooth. Heat the olive oil in a large saucepan over medium heat. Add the rice. Sauté for 5 minutes or until the rice is golden brown and crackling. Add the tomatillo mixture; mix well. Simmer, covered, for 40 to 45 minutes or until the liquid is absorbed and the rice is tender. Stir with a fork. Serve hot.

Serves 8

A sophisticated replacement for traditional Spanish rice.

Sage and Wild Rice Stuffing

With Kahlúa

Scott Tompkins
Marco Polo Café

1 pound whole pork sausage
1/2 rib celery, chopped
1/4 cup chopped yellow onion
Fresh thyme leaves
Fresh sage leaves
3 cloves of garlic, minced
2 cups cranberries, cooked
1 ounce Kahlúa
1 (1-pound) loaf white bread, cubed
4 cups cooked wild rice
Turkey stock
2 eggs, beaten

Brown the sausage with the celery and onion in a skillet over medium-high heat, stirring until the sausage is crumbly; drain well. Add the thyme, sage and garlic. Sauté for 2 minutes. Add the cranberries and Kahlúa. Sauté for 1 minute. Transfer the mixture to a large bowl; cool. Add the bread cubes and rice; mix well. Add enough turkey stock to moisten the mixture. Add the eggs; mix well. Chill the mixture until ready to stuff a 14- to 16-pound turkey.

Serves 8

Spinach Stuffing

2 tablespoons butter
1/2 cup chopped onion
3/4 cup melted butter
1 1/2 cups chicken broth
6 eggs, beaten
1 teaspoon thyme
2 tablespoons garlic salt
Pepper to taste
2 cups shredded Cheddar cheese
1 cup chopped pecans
2 (10-ounce) packages frozen chopped spinach,
thawed, drained
4 cups cubed herb stuffing mix
2 cups bread crumbs

Combine 2 tablespoons butter and onion in a skillet over medium-high heat. Sauté until the onion is soft. Combine 3/4 cup melted butter, broth, eggs, thyme, garlic salt, pepper and cheese in a bowl; mix well. Add the sautéed onions with their drippings and the pecans; mix well. Add the spinach, stuffing mix and bread crumbs; mix well. Transfer the mixture to a greased 11x14-inch baking dish. Bake at 325 degrees for 40 minutes.

Serves 10 to 12

Pacific Wave Wild Rice

1 cup pecan halves
3 1/2 cups chicken broth
1/4 cup sake or dry sherry
2 tablespoons light soy sauce
1/2 teaspoon Asian chili sauce
1/2 teaspoon salt
1 teaspoon grated orange peel
3 tablespoons unsalted butter
3 cloves of garlic, minced
1 1/2 cups wild rice
2/3 cup dried currants
1/2 cup minced green onions
1/2 cup packed cilantro sprigs or
fresh basil leaves, chopped

Spread the pecans on a baking sheet. Bake at 325 degrees for 15 minutes or until pecans are well toasted; cool and set aside. Combine the broth, sake, soy sauce, chili sauce, salt and orange peel in a small bowl; mix well. Melt the butter in a 2 1/2-quart saucepan over medium-high heat. Add the garlic. Sauté for 10 seconds. Add the rice. Sauté for 5 minutes. Add the currants and broth mixture; mix well. Bring to a boil, stirring occasionally. Reduce the heat. Cook, covered, for 45 minutes or until the rice is tender. Add extra water or broth toward the end of the cooking if the rice begins to scorch. Add the onions, cilantro and toasted pecans; mix well.

Serves 8

Festive Fruit Compote with

Cranberries

3 cups apple juice
I cup packed light brown sugar
2 (8-ounce) packages mixed dried fruit
I cup orange juice
$^1/_2$ cup raisins
6 slices lemon
6 orange sections
2 cinnamon sticks
I cup fresh or frozen cranberries
$^1/_2$ cup chopped walnuts

Combine the apple juice and brown sugar in a large saucepan over low heat. Cook until the brown sugar is dissolved, stirring frequently. Add the dried fruit, orange juice, raisins, lemon slices, orange sections and cinnamon sticks. Simmer for 30 minutes or until the fruit is tender, stirring occasionally. Add the cranberries. Simmer for 5 minutes or until the cranberries are cooked through but not popped. Remove from the heat; cool. Chill, covered, for 4 hours or until completely cooled. Add the walnuts; mix well.

Serves 10

A wonderful holiday brunch side dish.

Side Dishes

Desserts

Chocolate Citrus Cake

1 cup sugar
1/2 cup butter
1/4 cup orange liqueur
1/4 cup water
1 (2-layer) package devil's food cake mix
1 cup sour cream
1 (4-ounce) package chocolate fudge instant pudding mix
4 eggs
1/2 cup vegetable oil
1/2 cup water
1/4 cup coffee liqueur
2 tablespoons grated orange peel
1 teaspoon ground cinnamon
2 cups chocolate chips
Confectioners' sugar

Combine the sugar, butter, orange liqueur and 1/4 cup water in a saucepan over low heat; mix well. Cook for 3 minutes or until the butter is melted and the sugar is dissolved, stirring constantly. Bring to a boil. Remove from the heat; cool completely and set aside. Grease a 10-cup bundt pan and dust with baking cocoa. Combine the cake mix, sour cream, pudding mix, eggs, oil, 1/2 cup water, coffee liqueur, orange peel and cinnamon in a mixer bowl. Beat for 3 minutes on medium speed or until smooth. Fold in the chocolate chips. Pour the batter into the prepared pan. Bake at 350 degrees for 1 hour or until cake tests done. Remove cake from the oven. Spoon the cooled sugar mixture over the top immediately. Let the cake stand for 30 minutes. Turn out onto a serving platter. Cool completely. Sprinkle confectioners' sugar over the top.

Serves 10

Desserts

Flourless Chocolate Cake

Eddie Matney
Eddie Matney's Epicurian Trio

¹/₂ cup butter, softened
1 (8-ounce) package Oreo cookies, crushed
9 egg yolks
1¹/₂ pounds chocolate
5 tablespoons lime juice
¹/₄ cup honey
2 mangos, peeled, cut into ¹/₄-inch pieces
1 pint fresh strawberries, cut into ¹/₄-inch pieces
2 tablespoons chopped fresh mint leaves

Combine the butter and Oreo cookie crumbs in a bowl; mix well. Pat the mixture over the bottom of a 9-inch cake pan. Beat the egg yolks in a mixer bowl until thick and doubled in bulk. Melt the chocolate in the top of a double boiler. Remove from the heat; cool slightly. Fold the egg yolks into the chocolate. Pour the batter over the prepared crust. Place the cake pan in a larger shallow pan of hot water. Bake in the water bath at 350 degrees for 30 minutes. Remove the cake pan to a wire rack to cool for 5 minutes. Turn out onto the rack to cool completely. Combine the lime juice and honey in a bowl; mix well. Add the mangos, strawberries and mint leaves; mix well. Serve with the cake.

Serves 8 to 10

Holiday Cake with

Hard Sauce

1 (28-ounce) jar mincemeat with rum or brandy
1 cup sugar
2 egg yolks
1 teaspoon vanilla extract
1 cup pecan pieces
¹/₂ cup melted butter
1 cup raisins
2 cups flour
1 teaspoon baking soda
1 tablespoon boiling water
2 egg whites
¹/₂ cup unsalted butter, softened
1¹/₂ cups confectioners' sugar
2 tablespoons brandy, or to taste

Mix the first 7 ingredients in a mixer bowl. Add the flour a little at a time, mixing well after each addition. Dissolve the baking soda in the boiling water. Add to the flour mixture; mix well. Add the egg whites. Beat until well mixed. Pour into a greased bundt pan dusted with bread crumbs. Bake at 325 degrees for 1¹/₄ hours. Cool in the pan. Cream ¹/₂ cup butter and confectioners' sugar until light and fluffy. Stir in the brandy. Serve with the cake.

Serves 12 to 16

Desserts

Almond Black Bottom Cheesecake

1¹/₂ cups chocolate wafer crumbs
1 cup chopped toasted blanched almonds
¹/₃ cup sugar
6 tablespoons butter, softened
1 cup sugar
24 ounces cream cheese, softened
4 eggs
¹/₃ cup heavy cream
¹/₄ cup amaretto
1 teaspoon vanilla extract
2 cups sour cream
1 teaspoon vanilla extract
1 tablespoon sugar
Toasted slivered blanched almonds

Combine the wafer crumbs, chopped almonds, ¹/₃ cup sugar and butter in a mixer bowl; mix well. Press the mixture over the bottom and up the side of a buttered 9¹/₂- or 10-inch springform pan. Cream 1 cup sugar and cream cheese in a mixer bowl until light and fluffy. Beat in the eggs 1 at a time. Add the cream, amaretto and 1 teaspoon vanilla. Beat until the mixture is light and fluffy. Pour over the prepared crust. Bake at 375 degrees for 30 minutes. Cool on a wire rack for 5 minutes. Combine the sour cream, 1 teaspoon vanilla and 1 tablespoon sugar in a bowl, stirring until the sugar is dissolved. Spread over the cake. Return the cake to the oven. Bake for 5 minutes. Cool in the pan on a wire rack. Chill, covered, for 5 hours. Remove the side of the pan. Transfer the cake to a serving plate. Press the toasted slivered almonds around the top edge.

Serves 10 to 12

Chocolate Peanut Butter

Cheesecake

1¹/₂ cups chocolate wafer crumbs
1 tablespoon sugar
2 tablespoons melted unsalted butter
16 ounces cream cheese, softened
1¹/₂ cups sugar
²/₃ cup creamy peanut butter
5 eggs
¹/₂ cup sour cream
2 teaspoons freshly squeezed lemon juice
1 cup semisweet chocolate chips
1 cup sour cream
³/₄ cup melted semisweet chocolate chips
¹/₂ cup sugar

Mix the crumbs, 1 tablespoon sugar and butter in a mixer bowl. Press over the bottom and up the side of a greased 9-inch springform pan. Chill for 30 minutes. Process the cream cheese, 1¹/₂ cups sugar, peanut butter, eggs, ¹/₂ cup sour cream and lemon juice in a food processor until smooth. Fold in 1 cup chocolate chips by hand. Pour into the prepared crust. Bake at 350 degrees for 1 hour and 10 minutes to 1 hour and 20 minutes or until the center is firm. Cool on a wire rack for 15 minutes. Beat 1 cup sour cream, ³/₄ cup chocolate chips and ¹/₂ cup sugar in a mixer bowl until the sugar is dissolved. Spread over the top of the warm cheesecake. Return the cheesecake to the oven. Bake for 10 minutes. Cool on a wire rack for 1 hour. Chill for 3 hours before removing the side of the pan.

Serves 12

Desserts

Fairy Pie

1/2 cup butter, softened
1/2 cup sugar
4 egg yolks
2/3 cup flour
1/2 teaspoon salt
1 teaspoon baking powder
1/4 cup milk
4 egg whites
1/8 teaspoon cream of tartar
1 cup sugar
1 teaspoon vanilla extract
2 cups heavy cream
1 tablespoon sugar
1 teaspoon vanilla extract
1 to 2 cups crushed fresh fruit

Cream the butter and 1/2 cup sugar in a mixer bowl until light and fluffy. Add the egg yolks. Beat until light and fluffy. Mix the flour, salt and baking powder in a bowl. Add the flour mixture and milk alternately to the creamed mixture, mixing well after each addition. Pour into 2 greased and floured 8-inch round baking pans. Chill until the meringue is ready. Beat the egg whites and cream of tartar in a mixer bowl until stiff peaks form. Add 1 cup sugar and 1 teaspoon vanilla gradually, beating until stiff shiny peaks form. Spread the meringue over the batter, sealing the edges with meringue. Bake at 350 degrees for 20 to 25 minutes or until layers test done. Cool in the pans. Combine the cream, 1 tablespoon sugar and 1 teaspoon vanilla in a mixer bowl. Beat until soft peaks form. Fold in the crushed fruit. Spread between the layers and over the top of the dessert. Chill until ready to serve.

Serves 8 to 10

A Bavarian delight.

Desserts

Fruit Puff Tart with

Almond Cream

Tammie Coe
Desert Highlands

7 tablespoons almond paste
I egg, beaten
7 tablespoons sugar
7 tablespoons butter, softened
6 tablespoons cake flour
I sheet frozen puff pastry, thawed
I to 2 cups fresh fruit, any kind
I to 2 tablespoons sugar
I to 2 tablespoons butter

Cream the almond paste, egg, 7 tablespoons sugar and 7 tablespoons butter in a mixer bowl until smooth. Add the flour gradually, beating well after each addition. Cut the pastry into any shape you choose. Pierce the dough all over with a fork. Spread the almond cream over the dough to within $^1/_2$ inch of the edge. Arrange the fruit in a decorative pattern over the almond cream. Sprinkle I to 2 tablespoons sugar over the fruit. Dot with the I to 2 tablespoons butter. Bake at 400 degrees until the crust is brown around the edges and the juices from the fruit bubble.

Serves 6

Desserts

Lemon Almond Tart

1 cup unbleached flour
1 tablespoon sugar
1/4 cup sliced almonds
1/4 teaspoon salt
7 tablespoons cold unsalted butter,
   cut into pieces
1 tablespoon cold water
1/2 teaspoon almond extract

4 eggs
1 1/4 cups sugar
6 tablespoons lemon juice
2 tablespoons unsalted butter
2 tablespoons grated lemon peel
1/3 cup sliced almonds
Confectioners' sugar

Process the flour, 1 tablespoon sugar, 1/4 cup almonds and salt in a food processor until the mixture is the texture of coarse meal. Add 7 tablespoons butter 1 piece at a time, pulsing until the mixture is the texture of coarse meal. Add a mixture of the water and almond extract. Process until moist clumps form. Form the dough into a ball and flatten. Press the dough evenly over the bottom and up the side of a 9-inch tart pan with a removable bottom. Freeze for 30 minutes or until firm. Whisk the eggs and 1 1/4 cups sugar in a saucepan. Add the lemon juice and lemon peel. Cook over medium heat for 5 minutes or until thickened, whisking constantly; do not boil. Remove from the heat. Whisk in 2 tablespoons butter. Transfer the mixture to a bowl. Chill for 2 hours or until cold, stirring occasionally. Remove the crust from the freezer. Line the crust with foil and fill with pie weights or dried beans. Bake at 400 degrees for 15 minutes or until the crust is golden brown. Remove from the oven and cool completely. Reduce the oven temperature to 350 degrees. Spread the chilled lemon juice mixture on the cooled crust. Sprinkle with 1/3 cup almonds. Bake for 35 to 40 minutes or until the filling puffs slightly and begins to crack around the edges. The center should jiggle slightly. Cool on a wire rack. Remove the side from the tart pan. Sprinkle with confectioners' sugar before serving.

Serves 8

Desserts

Musician's Tart

1 1/4 cups flour
3 tablespoons sugar
1/8 teaspoon salt
1/2 cup cold unsalted butter,
cut into pieces
1 egg yolk
1/2 teaspoon vanilla extract
7 1/2 tablespoons heavy cream
1 cup chopped dried pears

1 cup pitted dates, halved
1/3 cup pear nectar
1/4 cup packed dark brown sugar
6 tablespoons unsalted butter, softened
6 tablespoons packed dark brown sugar
3 tablespoons light corn syrup
1/2 cup pine nuts
1/2 cup toasted whole almonds
1/2 cup dry roasted cashews

Process the flour, sugar and salt in a food processor until well mixed. Add 1/2 cup butter 1 piece at a time, pulsing until the mixture resembles coarse meal. Add the egg yolk and vanilla, pulsing until well mixed. Add 6 tablespoons of the cream 1 tablespoon at a time, pulsing after each addition until the dough begins to clump. Shape the dough into a ball and flatten. Wrap in plastic wrap. Chill for 30 minutes. Roll between 2 sheets of waxed paper into a 12-inch circle. Fit into a 9-inch tart pan with a removable bottom. Trim the edges. Freeze for 15 minutes. Line the crust with foil. Fill with pie weights or dried beans. Bake at 350 degrees for 10 minutes or until set. Remove the foil and weights. Bake for 20 minutes or until the crust is golden brown. Cool on a wire rack. Bring the pears, dates, pear nectar and 1/4 cup brown sugar to a boil in a saucepan over medium-high heat. Reduce the heat. Simmer for 1 minute. Process in a food processor until a thick paste forms; cool. Cook 6 tablespoons butter, 6 tablespoons brown sugar and corn syrup in a saucepan over low heat until the brown sugar is dissolved. Boil for 1 minute. Remove from the heat. Add the remaining 1 1/2 tablespoons cream, pine nuts, almonds and cashews; mix well. Spread the fruit filling evenly over the crust. Place the tart pan on a baking sheet. Spread the nut mixture over the filling. Bake at 400 degrees for 20 minutes or until the filling bubbles. Cool on a wire rack. Remove the side of the tart pan and cut the tart into wedges.

Serves 6

Raspberry Tart

Vincent Guerithault
Vincent's on Camelback

1/2 cup unsalted butter, softened
1/3 cup confectioners' sugar
10 egg yolks
3 3/4 cups flour
2 cups half-and-half

1/2 cup sugar
2 pints fresh raspberries
1 small jar raspberry or apricot jelly or preserves
1 tablespoon water

Cream the butter and confectioners' sugar in a mixer bowl until light and fluffy. Add 6 of the egg yolks 1 at a time, mixing well after each addition. Add 3 1/2 cups of the flour gradually, beating on low speed until thoroughly blended. Do not overmix. Chill the dough for 1 hour. Combine the half-and-half and the remaining 1/4 cup sugar in a saucepan over medium-high heat. Boil until the sugar is dissolved. Cream remaining 4 egg yolks and 1/4 cup sugar in a mixer bowl until light and fluffy. Add the remaining 1/4 cup flour gradually, mixing well after each addition. Add to the boiling half-and-half slowly, whisking constantly. Whisk until the mixture returns to a boil. Remove from the heat. Pour into a bowl; cool. Roll the dough 1/8 inch thick on a floured surface. Fit the dough into a tart pan. Bake at 350 degrees until golden brown. Cool completely. Spread the half-and-half mixture over the crust. Arrange the raspberries on top. Combine the jelly and water in a small saucepan over medium-high heat. Bring to a boil. Cook until the jelly is melted, stirring constantly. Remove from the heat. Drizzle 1 tablespoon of the jelly mixture around each slice of tart. Garnish with mint leaves.

Serves 8

A photograph of this recipe appears on the cover.

Desserts

Chocolate Malakoff

1/2 cup orange liqueur
2 packages ladyfingers
1 cup unsalted butter, softened
1 cup superfine sugar
2/3 cup semisweet chocolate chips
1/4 cup strong coffee
1/4 teaspoon almond extract
1 1/3 cups finely chopped almonds
2 cups heavy cream

Line the bottom and side of a springform pan with waxed paper. Sprinkle 1/2 of the orange liqueur over the ladyfingers. Arrange the ladyfingers rounded side out around the inside of the pan. Cream the butter and sugar in a food processor until light and fluffy. Add the remaining 1/2 of the orange liqueur. Cook the next 3 ingredients in a small saucepan over medium heat until the chocolate is melted, stirring frequently. Add to the creamed mixture. Process until the sugar is dissolved. Add the almonds; mix well. Whip the cream in a mixer bowl until soft peaks form. Fold into the chocolate mixture. Layer 1/3 of the chocolate mixture, 1/2 of the remaining ladyfingers, 1/2 of the remaining chocolate mixture, remaining ladyfingers and remaining chocolate mixture in the prepared pan. Cover with waxed paper. Chill for 6 hours. Unmold and garnish with whipped cream rosettes and shaved chocolate.

Serves 12

Rich and Crunchy

Chocolate Pie

4 ounces German's chocolate, melted
1/2 cup melted margarine or butter
3 eggs, beaten
1 cup sugar
1/2 cup flour
1 teaspoon vanilla extract
1/2 cup chopped pecans

Combine the chocolate and margarine or butter in a mixer bowl; mix well. Add the eggs and sugar. Beat until well mixed. Add the flour, vanilla and pecans. Beat until well mixed. Pour the mixture into a buttered pie pan. Bake at 325 degrees for 30 minutes.

Serves 6

Parnassiene au Chocolate

"*Chocolate Tower*"

Christopher Gross
Christopher and Paola's Fermier Brasserie

5¹/₂ ounces semisweet chocolate, broken into pieces
3 tablespoons sliced unsalted butter
¹/₄ cup heavy cream
10 egg whites
¹/₄ cup superfine sugar
3 ounces melted semisweet chocolate
6 ounces melted white chocolate
1¹/₂ cups half-and-half
¹/₂ vanilla bean, split, or 1 teaspoon vanilla extract
6 egg yolks
²/₃ cup sugar
1 cup espresso beans

Melt 5¹/₂ ounces chocolate and butter in a stainless steel bowl placed over simmering water, stirring occasionally. Cool to room temperature. Beat the cream in a stainless steel bowl set over a larger bowl of ice water until stiff peaks form. Beat the egg whites in a mixer bowl until soft peaks form. Add ¹/₄ cup sugar gradually, beating constantly until stiff peaks form. Whisk ¹/₄ of the egg whites into the chocolate mixture. Fold in the remaining egg whites. Fold in the whipped cream. Fold a 3¹/₂x5-inch piece of parchment paper into a cylinder 5 inches tall and 1¹/₂ inches in diameter. Close with tape. Make sure the cylinder will stand upright. Form a total of 8 cylinders. Fill a pastry bag with the chocolate mixture. Pipe into the cylinders, leaving a ¹/₂-inch space at the top. Drape plastic wrap over the tops of the cylinders. Freeze for 1 hour or until firm. Cut eight 5x5-inch pieces of parchment paper. Fill a decorating cone with some of the melted

Parnassiene au Chocolate

"Chocolate Tower"

3 ounces semisweet chocolate. Drizzle diagonal lines in a lattice pattern on each square. Place the squares on a baking sheet. Freeze for 5 minutes or until the chocolate is set. Remove 1 lattice at a time from the freezer. Spread 2 to 3 tablespoons of white chocolate in a very thin layer on top of the lattice, leaving a 1-inch strip on 1 side. Scrape off and discard any excess white chocolate. Unwrap 1 frozen mousse tower; place on top of the white chocolate, parallel to and opposite the uncoated strip. Wrap the parchment around the mousse quickly, leaving the uncoated flap overlapping. Return each finished tower to the freezer. Peel off and discard the papers after 5 minutes. The lattice will remain in place around the mousse. Defrost in the refrigerator for 1 hour before serving. Bring the half-and-half and vanilla bean to a simmer in a saucepan over medium heat. Remove from the heat; cover and set aside. Beat egg yolks in a saucepan until thick. Beat in 2/3 cup sugar gradually. Discard the vanilla bean. Whisk 1/4 cup of the hot mixture into the egg yolks; whisk the egg yolks into the hot mixture. Add the espresso beans. Cook over low heat until thick, stirring constantly. Strain through a fine sieve into a bowl. Serve warm, tepid or chilled. Serve with the mousse.

Serves 8

One of the most popular desserts in town, as seen on Julia Child's
PBS series In Julia's Kitchen with Master Chefs.

Vincent's Crème Brûlée in

Sweet Taco Shells

Vincent Guerithault
Vincent's on Camelback

1 1/2 cups heavy cream
1 cup sugar
1 vanilla bean, split
10 egg yolks, beaten
1/2 cup butter, softened
1 cup confectioners' sugar

4 egg whites
1 cup flour
2 cups assorted fresh berries, such as
strawberries, raspberries and
blueberries

Make the crème brûlée 24 hours before serving. Bring the cream, 3/4 cup of the sugar and vanilla bean to a boil in a heavy saucepan over high heat. Remove from the heat. Add the egg yolks, whisking constantly. Cook over low heat until thick enough to coat the back of a spoon, stirring constantly; do not boil. Transfer the custard to a stainless steel bowl set in a larger bowl of ice water. Stir constantly until the mixture is cool. Chill, covered, for 12 hours. Cream the butter and confectioners' sugar in a mixer bowl until light and fluffy. Beat in the egg whites slowly. Add the flour; beat until well mixed. Grease 2 baking sheets. Spoon the batter into four 3-inch circles, making sure the circles are not touching. Bake at 400 degrees for 7 minutes or until golden brown. Drape each circle immediately over the base of a 2-inch drinking glass. Cool the shells until stiff. Fill each shell with 1/2 cup of berries. Discard the vanilla bean and spoon the custard over the berries. Sprinkle each with 1 tablespoon sugar. Broil 4 inches from the heat source until the sugar is melted and caramelized. Be careful not to burn the edges of the shells. Serve immediately.

Serves 4

Desserts

Bread Pudding with

Drunken Sauce

6 jumbo croissants, torn into pieces
3 cups milk
1 cup heavy cream
3 eggs
1 1/2 cups packed light brown sugar
1/4 teaspoon nutmeg
1/2 teaspoon cinnamon
2 tablespoons vanilla extract

1 1/2 cups raisins
2 apples, peeled, chopped
2 tablespoon melted butter
1 egg, beaten
1/2 cup butter
1 cup confectioners' sugar
1/4 cup rum, bourbon or
amaretto

Combine the croissants, milk and cream in a large mixer bowl. Let stand for 30 minutes. Cream 3 eggs, brown sugar, nutmeg, cinnamon and vanilla in a mixer bowl until light and fluffy. Add to the moistened croissants; mix well. Fold in the raisins and apples. Pour the mixture into a greased 9x13-inch baking pan. Drizzle 2 tablespoons melted butter over the top. Bake at 325 degrees for 1 hour and 10 minutes. Combine 1 egg, 1/2 cup butter and confectioners' sugar in the top of a double boiler. Cook until thickened, whisking constantly. Remove from the heat. Stir in the rum. Serve over the bread pudding.

Serves 12

Who could resist this?

Desserts

Flan Fantastic

1 cup sugar
3 egg whites
8 egg yolks
2 (12-ounce) cans evaporated milk
³/4 cup sugar
2 teaspoons vanilla extract
2 tablespoons brandy or rum

Place 1 cup sugar in a deep heatproof square baking pan. Cook over medium heat until the sugar is dissolved and golden brown, stirring constantly. Remove the pan from the heat. Tilt the pan until the caramelized sugar coats the bottom of the pan completely. Set aside to cool. Combine the egg whites and egg yolks in a mixer bowl. Beat until well mixed. Add the evaporated milk, ³/4 cup sugar and vanilla. Beat until the sugar is dissolved. Strain the egg mixture into the caramel-coated pan. Cover the pan and place in a larger pan containing 1 inch of hot water. Bake in the water bath at 350 degrees for 1 hour. Remove from the oven and turn the custard out onto a serving platter. Pour brandy over the top. Ignite the brandy with a long match. Serve flaming.

Serves 8

Hot Fudge Sundae Sauce

1 cup chocolate chips
¹/2 cup butter
2 cups confectioners' sugar
1¹/3 cups evaporated milk
1 teaspoon vanilla extract

Combine the chocolate chips and butter in a saucepan over medium heat. Cook until the chocolate is melted, stirring frequently. Add the confectioners' sugar and evaporated milk; mix well. Bring to a boil, stirring constantly. Cook for 8 minutes at a rolling boil. Remove from the heat. Stir in the vanilla. Store in the refrigerator. Heat before serving.

Serves 12 to 16

Keeps well for months.

Lemon Dessert Sauce

1 cup sugar
1/2 cup freshly squeezed lemon juice
2 teaspoons grated lemon peel
3 eggs, beaten
1 cup heavy cream

Combine the sugar, lemon juice and lemon peel in the top of a double boiler. Cook until the sugar is dissolved, stirring frequently. Remove from the heat. Stir some of the hot sugar mixture into the eggs in a bowl. Add the eggs to the sugar mixture gradually, stirring constantly. Return the pan to the heat. Cook until thickened, stirring constantly. Chill completely. Whip the cream until soft peaks form. Fold into the cooled custard mixture. Refrigerate until ready to serve. Serve over berries or over pound cake.

Serves 8

Pink Grapefruit and Champagne Sorbet

Barbara Pool Fenzl
Les Gourmettes Cooking School

4 1/2 to 5 pounds pink grapefruit
1 cup sugar
1/4 cup dry Champagne (can be flat)

Squeeze 4 cups of juice from the grapefruit. Strain the juice into a bowl, pushing as much of the pulp through the strainer as possible. Combine the sugar and 1 cup of the juice in a saucepan over medium heat. Cook until the sugar is dissolved, stirring occasionally. Remove from the heat. Pour in the remaining juice. Add the champagne; mix well. Cool. Freeze in an ice cream maker using the manufacturer's directions. Serve with a little champagne poured over each serving. Garnish with a sprig of mint or candied violet.

Serves 6

Frozen Chambord Torte with

Raspberry Sauce

2 cups vanilla wafer crumbs
1 1/2 cups chopped slivered almonds
6 tablespoons melted unsalted butter
3/4 cup plus 2 tablespoons sugar
6 egg yolks
7 tablespoons Chambord liqueur
2 1/2 cups heavy cream

6 tablespoons confectioners' sugar
1 tablespoon vanilla extract
1 (12-ounce) package frozen
raspberries, thawed
Whole raspberries
Slivered almonds

Combine the vanilla wafer crumbs, chopped almonds, melted butter and 2 tablespoons sugar in a large bowl; mix well. Press the mixture over the bottom and up the side of a buttered 9x2 1/2-inch springform pan; set aside. Combine the egg yolks, 1/2 cup sugar and 6 tablespoons liqueur in a large bowl placed over boiling water; whisk until well mixed. Cook for 4 minutes or until thickened and creamy. Remove the bowl from the heat. Whisk for 5 minutes or until cool. Beat the heavy cream, confectioners' sugar and vanilla in a large mixer bowl until soft peaks form. Fold into the egg mixture. Pour the filling into the prepared crust. Freeze for 12 hours. Can be frozen, covered with plastic wrap, for 3 days. To make the sauce, combine the raspberries, remaining 1/4 cup of sugar and remaining tablespoon of liqueur in a blender container. Process until puréed. Chill, covered, until ready to use. Allow the torte to thaw for 10 minutes before cutting. Decorate the top of the torte with alternating rows of raspberries and slivered almonds. Swirl the raspberry sauce on a plate in a decorative pattern. Place a slice of the torte in the sauce. Spoon additional sauce over the torte. Garnish with a sprig of mint.

Serves 12 to 16

Desserts

Coconut Caramel Ring

2 tablespoons unflavored gelatin
1/2 cup cold water
1 cup hot milk
1 cup sugar
1/8 teaspoon salt
2 cups heavy cream, whipped
1 teaspoon vanilla extract
2 cups shredded coconut
1 cup packed light brown sugar
1 cup sugar
1 tablespoon flour
1 tablespoon butter
2/3 cup heavy cream

Combine the gelatin and cold water in a saucepan. Stir until the gelatin is softened. Add the milk, 1 cup sugar and salt; mix well. Cook over low heat until the sugar is dissolved; cool. Beat the mixture until fluffy. Fold in the whipped cream, vanilla and coconut. Pour the mixture into a ring mold. Chill for 12 hours or overnight. Combine the brown sugar, 1 cup sugar, flour, butter and 2/3 cup cream in a saucepan over medium heat. Cook until the brown sugar and sugar are dissolved, stirring constantly. Unmold the ring onto a serving plate and top with the brown sugar mixture. Serve additional whipped cream on the side.

Serves 8

Frozen Strawberry

Meringue Torte

1 cup graham cracker crumbs
1 cup plus 3 tablespoons sugar
1/4 cup melted butter or margarine
1/2 cup chopped pecans
3 cups whole strawberries
2 egg whites

1 tablespoon freshly squeezed
lemon juice
1 teaspoon vanilla extract
1/8 teaspoon salt
1/2 cup heavy cream

Combine the cracker crumbs, 3 tablespoons sugar, butter and pecans in a bowl; mix well. Press the mixture over the bottom of a 10-inch springform pan. Bake at 325 degrees for 10 minutes. Remove from the oven and cool completely. Slice enough strawberries to make 2 cups; reserve the rest for garnish. Combine the sliced berries, 1 cup sugar, egg whites, lemon juice, vanilla and salt in a mixer bowl. Beat for a few minutes on low speed to mix well. Increase the speed to high and beat for 15 minutes or until peaks form when the beaters are lifted out of the batter. Beat the cream in a mixer bowl until soft peaks form. Fold the whipped cream into the berry mixture. Pour the mixture into the cooled crust. Freeze, covered, for 12 hours or until firm. Remove the side of the pan. Arrange 7 halved berries around the edge. Cut the torte into wedges. Serve immediately with sliced berries.

Serves 10 to 12

Prepare a day before serving.

1/2 cup vegetable shortening
1/2 cup butter, softened
11/2 cups sugar
2 eggs
2 teaspoons vanilla or almond extract
21/2 cups flour
1/2 teaspoon baking powder
3/4 teaspoon salt

Cream the shortening, butter and sugar in a mixer bowl until light and fluffy. Add the eggs and vanilla; beat to mix well. Sift the flour, baking powder and salt in a bowl. Add to the creamed mixture gradually, mixing well after each addition. Chill the dough. Roll the dough into small balls the size of a walnut. Place on a greased cookie sheet about 2 inches apart. Flatten with the bottom of a smooth glass dipped in flour. Decorate each cookie with a cherry, nut or colored sugar. Bake at 400 degrees for 5 minutes or until the edges are light brown.

Serves 60

1 cup butter, softened
21/2 cups packed light brown sugar
1/2 cup sugar
1 tablespoon water
1 tablespoon plus 1 teaspoon vanilla extract
2 egg yolks
2 cups flour
1/8 teaspoon salt
2 (12-ounce) packages chocolate chips
4 egg whites
Miniature marshmallows, optional

Cream the butter, 1/2 cup brown sugar and sugar in a mixer bowl until light and fluffy. Add the water, 1 tablespoon vanilla and egg yolks; mix well. Add the flour and salt; mix well. Butter and flour an 8x16-inch baking dish. Press the mixture over the bottom of the dish. Sprinkle chocolate chips over the top. Beat the egg whites in a mixer bowl until stiff peaks form. Add the remaining 1 teaspoon vanilla and the remaining 2 cups brown sugar 1 tablespoon at a time, mixing well after each addition. Spread the mixture over the chocolate chips. Sprinkle marshmallows over the top. Bake at 350 degrees for 20 to 25 minutes. Brown the top under the broiler.

Serves 30 to 40

Cut these in small squares as they are richer than Onassis—original recipe . . . original comment.

Chocolate Butter Cream

Layered Cookies

1¹/2 cups graham cracker crumbs
1 cup finely chopped walnuts
1 cup plus 1¹/2 tablespoons unsalted
butter
¹/4 cup sugar
¹/3 cup unsweetened baking cocoa
1 egg, beaten

1 teaspoon vanilla extract
2 tablespoons powdered custard or
pudding mix
3 tablespoons milk
2 cups confectioners' sugar
4 ounces semisweet baking chocolate

Combine the cracker crumbs and walnuts in a food processor or blender container. Process until the texture of fine meal. Combine ¹/2 cup butter, sugar, cocoa, egg and vanilla in a saucepan over medium heat; mix well. Cook for 5 minutes or until the consistency of custard, stirring constantly. Combine the crumb mixture and custard mixture in a bowl; mix well. Press into an ungreased 7¹/2x12-inch pan. Place in the freezer while making the next layer. Cream ¹/2 cup butter and custard or pudding mix in a mixer bowl until light and fluffy. Add the milk and confectioners' sugar. Beat until creamy. Remove the first layer from the freezer. Spread the mixture over the first layer. Return to the freezer. Melt the remaining 1¹/2 tablespoons butter and the baking chocolate in a small saucepan over low heat. Spread the melted chocolate over the chilled buttercream layer. Work quickly as the chocolate will harden when it touches the cold buttercream. Slice the cookies into 1¹/2-inch squares. Store, covered, in the refrigerator for up to 3 weeks or in the freezer for up to 3 months.

Serves 40

Grand Chocolate Mint Squares

1 cup sugar
1¹/₂ cups plus 6 tablespoons butter, softened
1 cup flour
4 eggs
¹/₂ teaspoon salt
1 teaspoon vanilla extract
1 (16-ounce) can chocolate syrup
2 cups confectioners' sugar
2 tablespoons crème de menthe
6 ounces chocolate chips

Combine the sugar, 1 cup of the butter, flour, eggs, salt, vanilla and chocolate syrup in a mixer bowl; mix well. Pour into a greased 9x13-inch baking pan. Bake at 350 degrees for 30 minutes. Cool completely. Combine the confectioners' sugar, crème de menthe and ¹/₂ cup of the butter in a mixer bowl; mix well. Spread over the cooled brownies. Freeze for 10 minutes. Melt the chocolate chips and the remaining 6 tablespoons of butter in a saucepan over medium heat, stirring constantly. Remove from the heat and cool. Spread over the crème de menthe layer.

Serves 24

As good as candy.

Chocolate Sherry Cream Bars

4 ounces baking chocolate
1 cup butter
4 eggs
2 cups sugar
1 cup sifted flour
$^1/_2$ teaspoon salt
1 teaspoon vanilla extract
4 cups confectioners' sugar
$^1/_2$ cup butter
$^1/_4$ cup cream
$^1/_4$ cup dry sherry
1 cup chopped walnuts
1 (6-ounce) package chocolate chips
3 tablespoons water
$^1/_4$ cup butter

Melt the baking chocolate and 1 cup butter in a bowl over boiling water, stirring to mix well. Beat the eggs in a mixer bowl until light and pale yellow. Add the sugar gradually, beating well after each addition. Add the chocolate mixture, flour, salt and vanilla. Beat for 1 minute. Pour into a greased and floured 10x14-inch baking pan. Bake at 325 degrees for 25 minutes. Remove from the oven; cool. Cream confectioners' sugar and $^1/_2$ cup butter in a mixer bowl until light and fluffy. Add the cream and sherry gradually, beating well after each addition. Fold in the walnuts; mix well. Spread over the baked chocolate layer. Chill. Melt the chocolate chips with the water and $^1/_4$ cup butter in a bowl over boiling water; mix well. Drizzle the mixture over the filling. Chill until firm before cutting into bars.

Serves 36 to 48

Desserts

Ginger Chews

1/2 cup butter-flavored shortening
1 cup sugar
1 egg
1/4 cup molasses
2 teaspoons baking soda
1 2/3 cups flour
1 teaspoon salt
1 teaspoon cinnamon
1 teaspoon ginger
Sugar for rolling

Cream the shortening and sugar in a mixer bowl until light and fluffy. Add the egg and molasses; mix well. Sift the baking soda, flour, salt, cinnamon and ginger together in a bowl. Add the dry ingredients a little at a time to the creamed mixture, beating well after each addition. Shape the dough into 1-inch balls. Roll the balls in sugar and place on a cookie sheet. Bake at 350 degrees for 7 minutes. Bake longer for gingersnaps.

A popular variation of the old classic gingersnap.

Gingersnaps

1 1/2 cups butter, softened
2 cups sugar
2 eggs
1 cup (scant) molasses
4 cups flour
1/4 teaspoon salt
4 teaspoons baking soda
1 tablespoon cinnamon
1 tablespoon cloves
1 tablespoon ginger
Sugar for rolling

Cream the butter and sugar in a large mixer bowl until light and fluffy. Add the eggs and molasses; mix well. Combine the flour, salt, baking soda, cinnamon, cloves and ginger in a bowl; mix well. Add the dry ingredients a little at a time to the creamed mixture, beating well after each addition. Chill, covered with plastic wrap, for 2 to 3 hours or overnight. Remove the dough from the refrigerator. Place sugar for rolling in a shallow dish. Shape the dough into 1-inch balls. Roll in the sugar. Place on a nonstick cookie sheet. Bake at 350 degrees for 8 to 10 minutes. They will flatten as they cook. Remove cookies to a wire rack to cool. Store in a sealable container.

Serves 60

Lucy's Lace Cookies

¹/₂ cup melted butter
I egg
2 teaspoons vanilla extract
I cup rolled oats
I cup sugar
I teaspoon salt
I tablespoon sifted flour
¹/₄ teaspoon baking powder

Combine the butter, egg and vanilla in a mixer bowl; beat to mix well. Combine the oats, sugar, salt, flour and baking powder in a bowl; mix well. Add the dry ingredients a little at a time to the butter mixture, mixing well after each addition. Chill for 12 hours or overnight. Cover a cookie sheet with foil. Drop the cookie dough by half teaspoonfuls onto the cookie sheet, allowing room for the cookies to spread when baking. Bake at 325 degrees for 10 to 15 minutes or until light brown. Remove from the oven. Cool. Pull the foil from the cookies.

Serves 36 to 48

Delicious with fresh fruit or ice cream. Dip the edges in melted chocolate for added sophistication.

Ann's Lemon Bars

2 cups flour
¹/₂ cup confectioners' sugar
¹/₂ cup butter or margarine
4 eggs
2 cups sugar
¹/₃ cup lemon juice
¹/₄ cup flour
¹/₂ tablespoon baking powder

Sift 2 cups flour and ¹/₂ cup confectioners' sugar into a mixer bowl. Cut in the butter until the mixture clings together. Press into a greased 9x13-inch baking pan. Bake at 350 degrees for 20 to 25 minutes. Combine the eggs, sugar and lemon juice in a mixer bowl. Beat until light and fluffy. Sift ¹/₄ cup flour and baking powder into the egg mixture; mix well. Pour the mixture evenly over the baked crust. Bake for 25 minutes. Remove from the oven. Sprinkle with additional confectioners' sugar. Cool completely. Cut into bars.

Serves 30

A Junior League staple.

Overnight Macaroons

4 cups quick-cooking oats
2 cups packed light brown sugar
1 cup safflower oil
2 eggs, beaten
1 teaspoon salt
1 teaspoon almond or vanilla extract

Combine the oats, brown sugar and safflower oil in a mixer bowl; mix well. Let stand for 12 hours or overnight. Add the eggs, salt and flavoring; mix well. Drop by teaspoonfuls onto a buttered cookie sheet. Bake at 325 degrees for 15 minutes. Remove cookies immediately to a wire rack to cool.

Serves 36 to 48

Oatmeal Carmelitas

1 (14-ounce) package caramels
1/2 cup heavy cream
1 1/2 cups flour
1 1/2 cups rolled oats
1 1/2 cups packed light brown sugar
1 egg (optional)
1/2 teaspoon baking soda
1/2 teaspoon salt
3/4 cup unsalted butter, cut into pieces
12-ounces semisweet chocolate chips
1 cup chopped pecans or walnuts

Heat the caramels and cream in a saucepan over medium heat. Cook until the caramels are melted, stirring constantly. Process the flour, oats, brown sugar, egg, baking soda and salt in a food processor until well mixed. Add the butter. Pulse on and off until the mixture begins to clump. Press 1/2 of the mixture into a greased 9x13-inch baking pan. Bake at 350 degrees for 8 to 10 minutes. Scatter chocolate chips and nuts over the crust. Drizzle with the caramel mixture. Sprinkle the remaining crumb mixture over the top. Bake for 20 minutes or until golden brown around the edges. Loosen the edges from the sides of the pan. Cool completely. Cut into squares. Chill until firm. Store in the refrigerator.

Serves 20

A hit with men. Very rich, and delicious served with coffee.

Wrangler Ranger Cookies

1³/4 cups flour
1 teaspoon baking soda
1¹/2 teaspoons baking powder
¹/4 teaspoon salt
1 cup unsalted butter, softened
1 cup sugar
1 cup packed light brown sugar
2 eggs
1 teaspoon vanilla extract
1 cup sweetened flaked coconut
1 cup rolled oats
2 cups lightly crushed cornflakes
12 ounces butterscotch chips

Combine the flour, baking soda, baking powder and salt in a bowl; mix well. Cream the butter, sugar and brown sugar in a mixer bowl until light and fluffy. Add the eggs 1 at a time, mixing well after each addition. Stir in the vanilla. Add the flour mixture gradually, mixing well after each addition. Add the coconut and oats; mix well. Add the cornflakes and butterscotch chips; mix well. Drop by rounded tablespoonfuls 2 inches apart onto a greased cookie sheet. Bake at 350 degrees for 10 to 12 minutes or until golden brown and still chewy. Remove to a wire rack to cool completely.

Serves 60

A classic favorite.

Pecan Puffs

1 cup butter, softened
³/4 cup sugar
1 teaspoon baking soda
1¹/2 cups flour
¹/2 tablespoon vanilla extract
¹/2 cup finely chopped pecans

Cream the butter, sugar and baking soda for 15 minutes in a mixer bowl. Add the flour gradually, mixing well after each addition. Add the vanilla and pecans; mix well. Drop by rounded teaspoonfuls onto an ungreased cookie sheet. Bake at 300 degrees for 20 minutes. Do not brown. Remove to a wire rack to cool.

Serves 36

Rich and popular.

Squaw Peak Pumpkin Bars

4 eggs
1²/₃ cups sugar
1 cup vegetable oil
1 (16-ounce) can pumpkin
2 cups flour
2 teaspoons baking powder
2 teaspoons cinnamon
1 teaspoon salt
1 teaspoon baking soda
3 ounces cream cheese, softened
¹/₂ cup butter or margarine, softened
1 teaspoon vanilla extract
2 cups confectioners' sugar

Cream the eggs, sugar, oil and pumpkin in a mixer bowl until light and fluffy. Combine the flour, baking powder, cinnamon, salt and baking soda in a bowl; mix well. Add dry ingredients to the pumpkin mixture gradually, mixing well after each addition. Spread the batter in ungreased 10x15-inch jelly roll pan. Bake at 350 degrees for 25 to 30 minutes. Cool completely. Cream the cream cheese, butter, vanilla and confectioners' sugar in a mixer bowl until light. Spread over the cooled layer. Cut into bars.

Serves 24

A fall favorite.

Cowboy Caramel Corn

6 quarts air-popped popcorn
2 cups packed light brown sugar
¹/₂ cup corn syrup
1 cup butter
¹/₂ teaspoon baking soda
¹/₈ teaspoon cream of tartar

Place the popcorn in a large roasting pan. Heat in the oven just until warm. Combine the brown sugar, corn syrup and butter in a saucepan over medium-high heat; mix well. Bring to a boil. Boil for 5 minutes, stirring frequently. Remove from the heat. Add the baking soda and cream of tartar; mix well. Pour over the warm popcorn gradually, mixing constantly. Bake at 200 degrees for 1 hour, stirring after 30 minutes.

Serves 24

Munch...munch...munch.

Dedications

The Junior League of Phoenix would like to thank these members and friends for financial contributions in support of Reflections Under the Sun:

Robin Vitols
To honor my favorite cook, my mother, Connie Rodie, and my favorite sommelier, my father, Bill Rodie.

Megan Congleton
To honor my mother, Marilyn Stromquist Congleton. Thanks for sharing the fun of food and the joy of entertaining with me.

Posey Moore Nash
To honor Virginia "Ginger" Blaine Moore.

Gary, Janice, Elizabeth and Jacob Cary
To honor our mother and grandmother, Helen Yarbrough.

The Cookbook Creation Committee
To honor Robin Vitols for all of her leadership and work to produce the cookbook.

Alice Henderson
To honor my namesake and favorite person, Alice "Granny" Orcutt.

Cathy Boyd
To honor the 1998-99 Junior League of Phoenix Board of Directors.

Brenda Heuring Harris
To my short order cook, Stephen "Pete" Harris, the man who adds spice to my life!

Nancy Roach
Thank you Tom and Kelly for your love and support during my Junior League career.

Elizabeth Saba
To honor my family.

Becki Jo Deem
To honor the women who have shaped my life.

Kathryn Heitel Bamberl
Because of you, forever and always. My mom, Dorothy Taylor Heitel, and my late aunt, Margaret Taylor Hance.

Dr. Anthony E. DiTommaso, Lyda DiTommaso-Espinosa, Dr. Karl H. Espinosa
In memory of Mary DiTommaso, a loving and devoted wife and mother.

Randi Rummage
In memory of my mother, Jane Campbell.

Charlie, Woody and Scott Thompson
To Kay, our guardian angel and loving wife, mother and Junior League of Phoenix President 1997-98.

Robin Vitols
Commending the Cookbook Creation Committee on a job very well done.

Contributors

The Junior League of Phoenix wishes to thank all of those who contributed to this cookbook. Contributors of recipes from **Something New Under The Sun**, **Fiesta Under The Sun** and **Desert Treasures** are individually credited in those books. We especially thank those who provided new recipes and recommended favorites for **Reflections Under the Sun**:

Chaunci Aeed	Susan Davenport-Johnson	Margery Jenkins	Elizabeth Saba
Amy Anton	Michele Davis	Laura Jorden	Anne Spellman
Becky Babson	Lyda DiTommaso-Espinosa	Anne Kunkel	Tracy Spooner
Mary Barnes	Pat Elder	Pat Kupec	Patricia Simmons
Kelly Barnhart	Elise Ely	Cristina Lenko	Jacque Steiner
Nancy Bayless	Carolyn Evani	Pit Lucking	Meredith Stewart
Jeannie Beal	Marion Flynn	Mary Lou Lyding	Cary Thomas
Sandy Benash	Gloria Gold	Ginger Moore	Francesca Thomas
Shaun Bracken	Janie Grue	Posey Moore Nash	Laura Thomas
Jean Bush	Sue Harris	Mary O'Riley	Pam Thomas
Janice Cary	Alice Henderson	Priscilla Person	Robin Rodie Vitols
Dorothy Clarendon	Pat Hester	Ann Rich	Karen Vivian
Karen Clements	Jeannette Hollander	Crystal Rimsza	Pam Weyers
Heather Cole	Marty Hornaday	Connie Rodie	Shirley Winslow
Marilyn Congleton	Ruth Ann Hornaday	Rebecca Rodie	Barbara Young
Megan Congleton	Jeanne Hoxie	Karen Rogers	
Colleen Cookson	Sandy Jackman	Pam Ryan	

Acknowledgements

Thank you to Vincent Guerithault and William McKellar Photography for our cover artwork. Special thanks to Dennis Brydon, M.D. and Bill Rodie, past Chairs of the Phoenix Chapter of The International Wine and Food Society, for their wine suggestions.

Index

Reflections Under the Sun

**The Brightest Collection of Recipes from
the Junior League of Phoenix**
Junior League of Phoenix, Inc.
P.O. Box 10223
Phoenix, Arizona 85064

Please send me _____ copies of *Reflections Under the Sun* $19.95 each $ _____
Postage and handling for first book $ 4.00 each $ _____
(add $1.00 postage/handling for each additional book)

Total $ _____

_____
Name

_____
Street Address

_____
City   State   Zip

_____
Telephone Number

[   ] VISA   [   ] MasterCard
[   ] Check enclosed made payable to the Junior League of Phoenix, Inc.

_____
Account Number   Expiration Date

_____
Cardholder Name

_____
Signature

Photocopies will be accepted.